An Introduction to Business Accounts

John Harrison & Ron Dawber

Pitman.

PITMAN PUBLISHING LIMITED
128 Long Acre, London WC2E 9AN

Associated Companies
Pitman Publishing Pty Ltd, Melbourne
Pitman Publishing New Zealand Ltd, Wellington

© John Harrison and Ron Dawber 1984

First published in Great Britain 1984

British Library Cataloguing in Publication Data
  Harrison, John
    An introduction to business accounts.
    1. Bookkeeping
    I. Title   II. Dawber, Ron
    657'.2   HF 5635

ISBN 0 273 01995 3

Text set in 10 on 11 pt Imprint Roman
Printed and bound in Great Britain at The Pitman Press, Bath

Contents

Preface

An Introduction to Business Accounts is a practical activity book designed for students training for employment as accounts or wages clerks, as well as providing a sound preparation for basic level examinations such as RSA Stage I Book-keeping; BTEC General Module, An Introduction to Business Accounts; Pitman Examinations Institute (Elementary); GCE 'O' level Principles of Accounts, etc.

We have adopted a case-study approach, centring the text and many of the exercises around P Faulkner & Sons, a sole trader in the business of manufacturing and marketing camping equipment. The book is based on the principle that the study of accounts is more realistic when related to office procedures and, conversely, office procedures are more meaningful when the accounting aspects are understood. The approach seeks to integrate these two important subjects and help students to understand the function of business documents in supplying data for accounting records.

There is no doubt that student activities are most effective when realistic business situations are simulated and actual forms and business documents are used in the learning situation. The exercises are all of a practical nature, to give students practice in looking up information from business records, completing business documents and using the data from these sources to prepare ledger accounts and eventually to calculate profit and loss. The use of calculators, copywriter boards, accounting machines and computers will enhance the value of these exercises.

The topics have been graded in easy stages to help students to learn and gain a clear understanding of the subject. We have recognised the need to adapt conventional systems to computer techniques by including a unit covering the computerisation of purchases, sales and wages, but we have also been conscious throughout the book of the need to give students a thorough grounding in the principles of accounts, which are essential for both fully computerised offices as well as those still operating manual systems.

The modern accounting format of using columns for debit, credit and balance has been used throughout the text, and in order to make the balances clearer to the student during the period of accounting training, we suggest that all final entries in accounts containing credit balances should be indicated by a 'Cr' and all other balances, ie the majority for assets and expenses, should be assumed to be debit.

In order to simplify the writing of this text the masculine pronoun has been used, but it should be made clear that all references to men apply equally to women and a deliberate distinction between the sexes is not implied.

Abbreviated answers are given on pages 148 to 150 for the first two exercises of each unit, as a guide to students on the accuracy of their work.

We hope that the experience students gain from working through the exercises in *An Introduction to Business Accounts* will be enjoyable and, at the same time, will help them to gain an understanding of accounting principles and practice.

RD & JH

Acknowledgments

The authors and publisher would like to thank the Royal Society of Arts for permission to reproduce questions from past examination papers, and the Midland Bank plc and Anson Systems for documents reproduced. The forms on pp 125 and 127 are Crown copyright and are reproduced with the permission of the Controller of Her Majesty's Stationery Office.

1 Introduction

The accounting and office procedures of a firm of camping equipment manufacturers, P Faulkner & Sons, form the central theme of this book. Whilst the systems outlined apply to Faulkners, the reader should appreciate that businesses adopt procedures which suit their own particular needs and no two will necessarily use the same. However, the principles remain the same.

Peter Faulkner started his business as a hardware merchant as long ago as 1949, when he came out of the Royal Air Force. By 1964, with the rapid increase in car ownership and the growing popularity of camping he had become involved with selling and hiring camping equipment.

At the present time Peter Faulkner's two sons, Simon and David, assist him in running the business, which now manufactures the 'Faulkner' range of tents and accessories. The sons receive a salary as employees, whilst they are learning the business, and expect to become partners or directors in about three years' time, when it is hoped that the present sole trader business will be converted into either a partnership or a limited company. Simon is currently studying to qualify for membership of the Institute of Chartered Secretaries and Administrators, whilst David hopes to sit the finals of the Institute of Cost and Management Accountants exam next year. Their duties are shown in the organisation chart (Fig 1) drawn up with the long-term plan of dividing the work as the business grows.

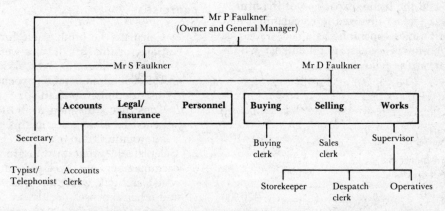

Accounts	Legal/ Insurance	Personnel	Buying	Selling	Works
Recording and controlling the financial affairs of the firm, including buying, selling, wages, etc. Calculation of profit and balance sheet. Costing. Budgetary control.	Liaison with solicitor regarding legal affairs of the firm. Control of insurance policies.	Recruitment, employment and dismissal of staff. Staff records. Welfare. Training. Staff conditions.	Negotiations with suppliers for purchase of goods and materials. Records of suppliers. Importing procedures.	Advertising. Market Research. Customer records. Home and export sales, including invoicing, transport and shipping. Sales service, including complaints and returns. Employment of representatives and agents.	Production of goods. Quality control. Design and development. Work study. Stores administration – stock control. Despatch of goods. Maintenance of equipment.

Fig 1   Organisation chart of P Faulkner & Sons

By keeping accounts for business transactions the firm has the necessary information to:

a determine the amount of profit or loss for a year or other period
b calculate the cost of manufacturing its commodities (camping equipment in the case of Faulkners)
c know what its customers (debtors) owe to the firm as well as its indebtedness to its suppliers (creditors)
d be aware of its cash position at any time
e draw up a balance sheet which reveals the firm's possessions (assets), debts (liabilities) and the amount invested in the firm by the owner (capital)
f conform with the legal requirements for wages and value added tax

Profit is the excess of revenue (income from sales) over the costs of manufacture and overheads, as explained below. The amount of revenue received is important to the employees of the firm so that they can receive adequate wages, bonuses, pensions and benefits such as canteen and social amenities. It also provides for replacement of machinery and the future expansion of the firm.

The major factors involved in calculating profit for a small business operating as a sole trader, as shown in the annual accounts of P Faulkner & Sons for last year, are as follows:

Profit calculation

	£	£
Revenue (Sales)		200 000
Less Materials	60 000	
Wages	60 000	
Admin expenses*	40 000	
Distribution costs*	10 000	
Total costs		170 000
Profit		£30 000

* Administration expenses are known as overheads. They include such items as telephone charges, stationery, lighting and heating, and rates. Distribution costs include the cost of transport of goods to customers, sales commission and advertising.

The following diagram illustrates the way in which £1 of sales was used by Faulkners last year:

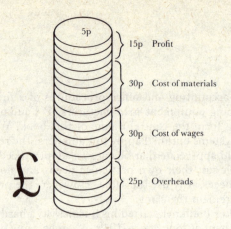

5p

15p Profit

30p Cost of materials

30p Cost of wages

25p Overheads

£

Exercises

1 a Calculate the profit made for P Faulkner & Sons for this year if sales were £250 000 and the costs were: wages £65 000, materials £65 000, administration expenses £50 000 and distribution costs £20 000.
  b Construct a diagram to illustrate what happened to £1 of sales in this year, using the information from a above.

2 Calculate the profit for your group of students if each member sold two articles at £10 each. The costs per article were: wages £2, materials £2.50 and other expenses £3.50.

3 Design a chart similar to the one illustrated above to show how your own weekly wages or allowances are used.

4 In which departments of a firm would you expect the following staff to be employed?
  a storekeeper   d order clerk
  b canteen staff   e shipping clerk
  c cost clerk

2 Buying

2.1 Requisitions and stock control

All materials used in the manufacture of camping equipment are stored in numbered bays in a stock room. The quantity in stock for each item is recorded on individual stock control cards (Fig 2). In this example 300 metres of tent cloth were in stock at 1 July.

Before any materials can be taken from the stock room a stores requisition must be made out (Fig 3, p 4). It is an instruction to the storekeeper to release the items listed.

The stores requisition must be signed by the works supervisor and the operative who receives the materials must also sign it. A copy of the requisition may be passed to the Costing Section to enable them to check the price being charged for the article. The storekeeper initials the requisition after handing over the stock items to the operative, and the issue is recorded on the stock control card. This reduces the balance so that it agrees with the quantity remaining in the stock room. For example, on 1 July, 300 metres of grade A gold tent cloth were in stock; 100 metres were taken out of the stores, as required by stores requisition No 734,

and the new balance of 200 metres was entered on the stock control card.

The stock control card shows the maximum and minimum quantity of stock. The firm does not wish to hold too much stock because this means that more money has to be paid out than is necessary and there is not a great deal of storage space available. On the other hand, it is essential that there are always sufficient materials to keep the workshop going for at least one month, and care must be taken to prevent any item falling to such a low quantity that it is impossible to order and receive new stock in time to continue production. A minimum stock figure is given to provide the storekeeper with a danger signal, and as soon as stocks drop to this level the item has to be replenished by means of a purchase requisition, similar to the stores requisition, but used by the storekeeper when buying goods.

A computer or a word processor using a record processing package can be used to maintain stock records; they have the minimum and maximum levels stored in their memories. When receipts and issues are entered on the keyboard, the balance of stock is automatically updated and the screen

STOCK CONTROL CARD

Description ....Grade A tent cloth (gold).... Bay No .....13...........
Code No ....60 TC A/G................ Maximum ....500 metres...........
                                         Minimum ....100 metres............
Normal quantity to order ......200 metres.... Ordering Level ..150 metres.......

| Date | Receipts | | Issues | | Balance in stock | Remarks |
	Goods rec'd note No	Quantity	Reqn No	Quantity		Goods on order and audit check
19–		metres		metres	metres	
July 1					300	
July 4			734	100	200	
July 14			823	100	100	5/7 Order No 97324
July 15	7 629	200			300	

Fig 2   Stock control card

Stores Requisition for Stock					No. 734

Materials Required for:

Date ....4/7/–....

Job No.............................Run No.....4321.............

Quantity	Description	Price per unit		Cost		Notes
		£	p	£	p	
100 metres	Code No 60 TC A/G Grade A tent cloth (gold)					

Works supervisor ....P long...........

Storekeeper's initials

Cost office ref:

Operative ....S Mills............

Fig 3   Stores requisition

shows the operator when the stock falls to the minimum figure, thus indicating the need for reordering. Stock valuations can also be seen and/or printed out as stock prices are stored on disc.

An effective stock control system should enable the firm to:

a keep an accurate check on the quantities issued (and avoid pilferage)
b ensure that production is not stopped (this would happen if the stores ran out of stock)
c minimise the space occupied by stock
d avoid deterioration or goods becoming obsolescent

Exercises

1 Prepare stores requisitions for tent zips (size 2 metres), code no 35 TZ, issued from stores on the following dates:

Aug	4	Quantity: 60	Job No 5861
	7	Quantity: 30	Job No 5920
	15	Quantity: 50	Job No 6004
	20	Quantity: 40	Job No 6102

Allocate appropriate requisition numbers.

2 Enter the stores requisitions prepared in Exercise 1 on a stock control card and calculate the balance after each transaction. The balance of stock on 1 August was 480. The stock levels were: maximum 500, minimum 200, ordering level 300 and normal quantity to order 240. The stock is held in bay no 15.

3 Rule up a stock control card for 'Empress' table lamps in ivory and gold colour with matching shade. The stock levels were: maximum 300, minimum 100, ordering level 150 and normal quantity to order 100.

Enter the following transactions extracting a balance after each entry:

Jan	1	Balance in stock 250
	6	20 drawn on Requisition No 802
	10	12 drawn on Requisition No 821
	15	40 drawn on Requisition No 850
	21	12 drawn on Requisition No 881

4 a Complete a stock control card with the following information:

Description: Spring-loaded plungers 1 cm (boxes of 500)
Supplier: Darling & Son Ltd
Max: 100 boxes, Min: 30 boxes
In stock on 8 February 19—: 55 boxes

			Reqn No
Feb	9	issued 5 boxes	439
	10	issued 3 boxes	443
	14	issued 10 boxes	449
	16	received 60 boxes from Darling & Son Ltd, Inv No 8745	
	17	issued 5 boxes	451
	20	issued 4 boxes	463

b Why was it desirable that 60 boxes should be received in the storeroom by 16 February?

2.2 Orders

The storekeeper has a standing instruction to make out a purchase requisition to replenish stock as soon as the quantity of any materials in stock falls to the ordering level. It is submitted for approval to the buyer who decides which supplier should be given the order. The buyer keeps an index of approved suppliers for the various materials required, and Fig 4 is an extract of the strip index kept by Faulkners for this purpose. (This index contains information for the various examples and exercises which follow.)

Material Suppliers Index	
Material	Suppliers
Aluminium tubing	NKG plc, Hall Lane, Sheffield, Yorks SD5 3AP
Brass sheeting	NKG plc, Hall Lane, Sheffield, Yorks SD5 3AP
Foam	Insulation Supply Co Ltd Albert Street, Kettering Northants KG8 6ML
Kapok filling	Insulation Supply Co Ltd, Albert Street, Kettering Northants KG8 6ML
Latex	Insulation Supply Co Ltd, Albert Street, Kettering Northants KG8 6ML
Netting (nylon)	Tape Works Ltd, Nette Lane, Nottingham NM1 8OR
Nylon (proofed)	CIC plc, Lanchester, Co Durham DM4 9SA
Nylon sheeting	CIC plc, Lanchester, Co Durham DM4 9SA
PVC	CIC plc, Lanchester, Co Durham DM4 9SA
PVC (nylon reinforced)	CIC plc, Lanchester, Co Durham DM4 9SA
Springs	Fettlenold & Sons, Birch Lane, Birmingham B29 2BR
Steel rods	Fettlenold & Sons, Birch Lane, Birmingham B29 2BR
Tape	Tape Works Ltd, Nette Lane, Nottingham NM1 8OR
Tent cloths	Outdoor Fabrics plc, Manchester Road, Bolton, Lancs BN3 2BT
Terylene filling	Insulation Supply Co Ltd, Albert Street, Kettering, Northants KG8 6ML
Thread	Sam Beller & Sons, Pickwick Works, Church Bank, Bradford, Yorks BD4 1AW
Twine	Sam Beller & Sons, Pickwick Works, Church Bank, Bradford, Yorks BD4 1AW
Zips (tent)	Darling & Son Ltd, Mawney Road, Romford, Essex RD7 2OP

Fig 4   Strip index of materials/suppliers

The completed purchases requisitions are passed to the typist to type a purchases order (see Fig 5). The information supplied in this purchases order is extracted from the purchases requisition and the supplier's price list (Figs 6 and 7). You will see that the order number incorporates the purchases requisition number 4321, and is entered on the purchases requisition after typing the order.

Five copies of the purchases order are prepared, for the reasons indicated in the diagram on p 7.

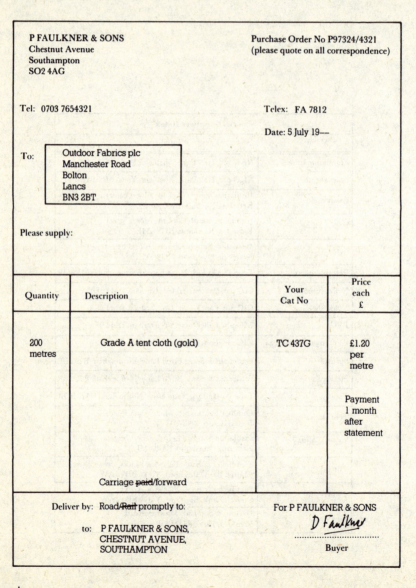

P FAULKNER & SONS
Chestnut Avenue
Southampton
SO2 4AG

Purchase Order No P97324/4321
(please quote on all correspondence)

Tel: 0703 7654321

Telex: FA 7812

Date: 5 July 19—

To:
Outdoor Fabrics plc
Manchester Road
Bolton
Lancs
BN3 2BT

Please supply:

Quantity	Description	Your Cat No	Price each £
200 metres	Grade A tent cloth (gold)	TC 437G	£1.20 per metre
			Payment 1 month after statement
	Carriage ~~paid~~/forward		

Deliver by: Road/~~Rail~~ promptly to:

to: P FAULKNER & SONS,
CHESTNUT AVENUE,
SOUTHAMPTON

For P FAULKNER & SONS

D Faulkner
....
Buyer

Fig 5 Purchases order

Purchases Requisition				No 4321
				Date....1 July 19--......

Quantity	Description	Supplier's Cat No	Purchase Order No	Supplier
200 metres	Grade A tent cloth (Gold)	TC437G	97324	Outdoor Fabrics plc

Signed.....*J Stockwell*..........Storekeeper   Approved.....**DF**.................
                                                              Buyer

Fig 6   Purchases requisition

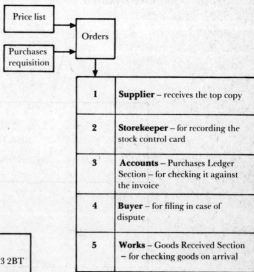

1	**Supplier** – receives the top copy
2	**Storekeeper** – for recording the stock control card
3	**Accounts** – Purchases Ledger Section – for checking it against the invoice
4	**Buyer** – for filing in case of dispute
5	**Works** – Goods Received Section – for checking goods on arrival

Price List

OUTDOOR FABRICS PLC, 90 MANCHESTER ROAD, BOLTON, LANCS BN3 2BT

Cat No	Description	Price (ex-warehouse)
S800	Grade A1 tent cloth – supplied in blue, gold, green and orange (width: 1 metre)	£1.20 per metre
S801	Grade A2 tent cloth – supplied in blue, gold, green and orange (width: 1 metre)	£1.05 per metre
S802	Grade A3 tent cloth – supplied in blue, gold, green and orange (width: 1 metre)	90p per metre
S803	Extra strong tarpaulin – supplied in blue and green (4 metres×4 metres)	£60
S804	Extra strong tarpaulin – supplied in blue and green (4 metres×5 metres)	£72
S805	Extra strong tarpaulin – supplied in blue and green (4 metres×6 metres)	£84
S806	Canopy with Grade A1 tent cloth – supplied in orange, green and blue (2 metres×4 metres)	£120
	Note: All prices exclude VAT	

Fig 7   Price list

Exercises

1 Refer to the price list on p 7 and prepare a purchases requisition for 100 metres of grade A2 green tent cloth. Allocate an appropriate requisition number.
2 Write or type a purchases order from the information supplied in the purchases requisition prepared for Exercise **1** and the price list on p 7. Allocate an appropriate order number and request rail transport.
3 Refer to the price list on p 7 and prepare a purchases order for the following items:

Cat No	Quantity required
S804	3
S806	2

These are required urgently, and delivery should be by road transport to P Faulkner & Sons at their Southampton address.

2.3 Goods received

When goods arrive at the loading bay, the driver hands over two copies of a delivery note or consignment note (Fig 8). One is for signature by the receiving clerk and is returned to the driver, the other is retained as a record of the delivery.

There are standing instructions that no one except authorised personnel may sign a delivery note, and then only if the correct number of packages are present and they are not damaged in any way.

Delivery Note

BOLTON CARRIERS LIMITED

Cheshire Road, Bolton, Lancashire
BN4 3AL

Delivered to:	P Faulkner & Sons Chestnut Avenue Southampton
By order of:	Outdoor Fabrics plc Manchester Road Bolton
Date despatched:	15 July 19—

Number of packages	Description	Comments
4 rolls (50 metres each)	Tent cloth	Ref Order No P97324/ 4321 dated 5/7/19—

Received in good order and condition

Customer's signature......T Jones......

Fig 8   A delivery note

Goods Received Note			No 7629	
Supplier: Outdoor Fabrics plc Manchester Road, Bolton BN3 2BT			Date: 15/7/19—	
Quantity	Description		Order No	
200 metres	Grade A tent cloth (Gold)		P97324/4321	
Carrier Bolton Carriers Ltd	Received by L Stone	Checked by J Stockwell	Bay No 13	
Condition of goods: Satisfactory/~~Unsatisfactory~~				
Distribution: Accounts ✓ Storekeeper Buyer				

Fig 9   Goods received note

A goods received note has to be made out in triplicate by the clerk in the Goods Received Section, but copies are not distributed until the goods have been checked in, and signed for, by the storekeeper. The goods received note no 7629 (Fig 9) has been completed for the tent cloth ordered in Fig 5.

Copies are distributed as follows:

1 **Accounts** (Purchases Ledger Section) to await the arrival of the invoice and provide evidence of the safe arrival of the goods
2 **Storekeeper** for entering the receipt of goods on the stock control card to record the new stock position (now 300 metres) as shown in Fig 2
3 **Buyer** to attach to his copy of the order

```
                    Delivery Note

                SPEEDFORDS LIMITED

            Snowhill Place, Aston, Birmingham
                        B15 1BT
```

Delivered to:	P Faulkner & Sons, Chestnut Avenue, Southampton
By order of:	Fettlenold & Sons, Birch Lane, Birmingham 29
Date despatched:	15 July 19——

Number of packages	Description	Comments
2 (50 in each)	Steel rods	Ref Order No S19874/333 dated 8/7/19——

Received in Good Order and Condition

Customer's Signature................ *J Baker* ....

Exercises

1 Complete a goods received note to record the receipt of the tent cloth ordered in Exercise **2** of Section 2.2 (p 8).
2 Prepare a goods received note for the goods delivered with the delivery note above.
3 Rule up a stock control card for terylene filling and enter the following details:

Max 800 kilos, Min 200 kilos
Ordering level: 250 kilos

July 1	Balance in stock	400 kilos
7	Requisition No 934	100 kilos
10	Requisition No 1023	100 kilos
14	Purchases Order No 97394	300 kilos
28	Goods Received Note No 7847	
		300 kilos
31	Requisition No 1079	50 kilos

4 *a* From the following information for April 19— relating to component XYZ you are to complete a stock card.

At 1 April the opening stock was 250 units. On 30 April it was discovered that there was a stock loss of 30 units.

Date	Requisition No	Issues	Receipts
Apr 3	K 14	42	
15	K 126	40	
18			100 Invoice 7321
20			6 Returns (RN176)
21	K 176	126	
28			50 Invoice 7328
29	K 190	80	

b How could you verify that the records were correct on 30 April 19—? (*RSA BKI*)

3 Accounts – Purchases Ledger Section

3.1 Purchases invoice procedure

When goods are bought the supplier provides the details, the terms and cost involved by means of an invoice similar to the one in Fig 10.

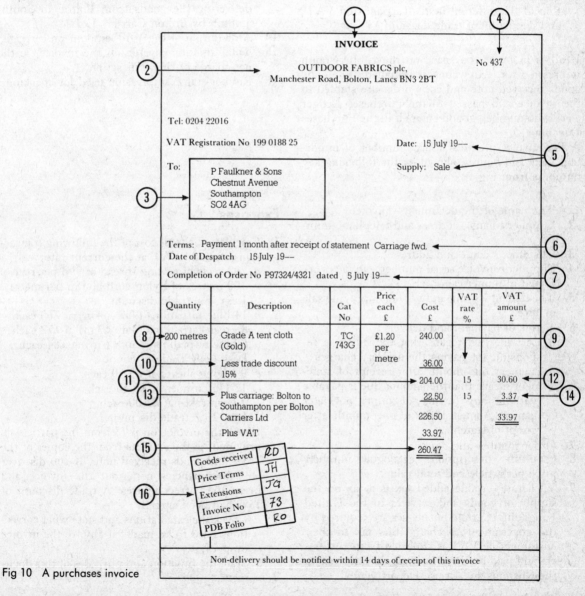

Fig 10   A purchases invoice

As soon as the invoice is received at Faulkner's accounts office the following procedure is adopted:

1 A rubber-stamp impression is made on the invoice to help with checking and to establish who has carried out the work. The invoice in Fig 10 has already been stamped.
2 A check is made to ensure that the goods have arrived, by extracting the copy of the appropriate goods received note from the file.
3 The price and terms are checked with the copy of the order in the copy order file.
4 The extensions are checked. (Extensions are the various calculations such as the quantity of goods multiplied by the rate per article; addition of the different items, carriage and VAT; and deduction of trade discount.)

If all is in order the space on the rubber-stamp impression for 'Extensions' is initialled. The copy goods received note and copy order are stapled to the invoice and passed to the Purchases Ledger clerk who numbers it and enters it in the Purchases Day Book.

The invoice provides a large number of important facts and figures, shown by the following key numbers from Fig 10.

1 The name of the document – invoice.
2 Supplier's name, address and telephone number.
3 Customer's name and address.
4 Supplier's invoice serial number – invoices are issued in numerical order.
5 The date of issuing and type of supply, ie sale or hire.
6 Terms of payment and delivery:
   a Carriage fwd means that the buyer is responsible for paying the delivery charges.
   b Payment one month after receipt of statement means that the amount due is payable (without any further discount) not later than 31 August 19—, ie one month after receipt of statement.
7 Order number and date.
8 Quantity, description, catalogue number, price per article and total value.
9 VAT rate – value added tax is a tax on the supply of goods and services in the United Kingdom. (Certain businesses are required by the government to charge this tax to their customers, ie VAT is collected from customers and paid by the firm at regular intervals to the Customs and Excise Department.)

10 Deduction of trade discount at 15% – an allowance made by Outdoor Fabrics plc to P Faulkner & Sons as a concession for trade within the industry. Trade discount might also be allowed for large orders, adjustment of list prices or an agent's profit. It should not be confused with cash discount which is associated with prompt payment.
11 The net value of goods purchased, ie the amount recorded in the accounts.
12 An addition of the VAT amount, ie 15% for the purpose of this book (but whatever the applicable rate is at the time) of the net value of the goods.
13 An addition for carriage, being the cost of delivering the goods from Bolton to Southampton by Bolton Carriers Ltd.
14 An addition of the VAT amount on carriage.
15 Total amount payable on the invoice, ie the net charge of this transaction.
16 Rubber-stamp impression used for checking.

Exercises

1 Calculate the total cost of the following transactions and add VAT at the current rate:
   a 200 reels of sewing thread at 99p per reel
       100 metres of nylon cord at 18p per metre
       Less 7½% trade discount
   b 14 blue tarpaulins (4 m × 4 m) at £60 each
       8 green tarpaulins (4 m × 5 m) at £72 each
       6 blue tarpaulins (4 m × 6 m) at £84 each
       Less 12½% trade discount
   c 9 edging shears at £9.50 each
       12 Dutch hoes at £6.40 each
       4 lawn rakes at £7.00 each
       Less 10% trade discount
2 Check the invoice on p 13 from the particulars provided, ie the extracts from the copies of the order and goods received note. If you discover any discrepancies copy out the invoice and insert the correct figures. A trade discount of 15% had been agreed.
3 *a* Check the calculations and state what corrections need to be made, if any, to the invoice on p 14.
   b State the function and purposes of this document.

INVOICE

FETTLENOLD & SONS

No 4926

Birch Lane, Birmingham B29 2BR

Tel: 021 493 6892

Telex: 893462

VAT Registration No 3043739 11

Date: 26 August 19–––

To:

P Faulkner & Sons
Chestnut Avenue
Southampton SO2 4AG

Supply: Sale

Date of
Despatch: 24 August 19–––

Terms: Delivered Southampton
Payment 2 months after invoice

Completion of Order No P97429/7624

Quantity	Description	Cat No	Price each £	Cost £	VAT rate %	VAT amount £
320 *230*	2 metre 5m/m diam steel rods	SR217	£1.45 per rod *1.54*	464.00		
	Less trade discount 15%			69.60		
				394.40	15	59.16
	Plus VAT			59.16		
				453.56		

Extract of Goods Received Note No 7726

Supplier: Fettlenold & Sons
Birmingham 15

Date: 24 August 19–––

Quantity	Description	Order No
230	2 metre 5 m/m diam steel rods	P97429/7624

Extract of Order No   P97429/7624

To: Fettlenold & Sons
Birmingham 15

Date: 16 August 19–––

Quantity	Description	Your Cat No	Price
230	2 metre 5m/m diam steel rods	SR217	£1.54 per rod delivered Southampton

Invoice

Stationery Supplies plc

No 34911

105 Park Crescent
Erith
Kent ER8 1AP

To: Fuller, Brightwell & Co Ltd
East Place
Liverpool L12 3CC

1 January 19—

Customer's order No PR 45863	Date of despatch 1/1/19—	Price per unit of 10	£	£
100 pocket files, brown		£1.50	15.00 ✓	
60 exercise books, brown		£1.10	6.00 ✗ 6·00	
200 biros		60p	12.60 ✗ 12·00	
50 shorthand notebooks		£1.80	9.00 ✓	
30 HB pencils		75p	2.50 ✗ 2·25	
			45.10 44·85	
Less 10%			4.51 4·49	
				49.61
20 reams bond typewriting paper		£22.00	44.00 ✓ 40 36	
Less 5%			4.40 2·20 41·80	
				39.60
		Total	89.21 82·16	
Add VAT at 15%			13.38 12·32	
		Net Total	102.59 94·48	

Consigned to: Address as above

3.2 Purchases Day Book and Ledger

The Purchases Ledger clerk receives the incoming purchases invoices after they have been checked. Numbers are allocated to them and entered in the space provided by the rubber stamp. They provide the data for entering, either manually, or by computer, in the Purchases Day Book or other record serving the same purpose.

The Purchases Day Book is a book of original entry as it is compiled from the original invoices received and contains a record of all goods purchased on credit for resale. It is not used for entering purchases paid for immediately in cash or for the purchase of goods which are not due to be sold as part of the firm's normal business.

The figures from the Purchases Day Book are transferred to the credit column of the suppliers' personal accounts in the Purchases Ledger. An account is a record of all the transactions relating to a person with whom business is conducted or to impersonal items affecting the running of a business such as machinery, rent, VAT, etc. At the end of the month the Purchases Day Book is totalled vertically and horizontally, providing a means of cross-casting, ie double checking that the individual transactions (horizontal) as well as the totals (vertical) are correct. This is illustrated in the

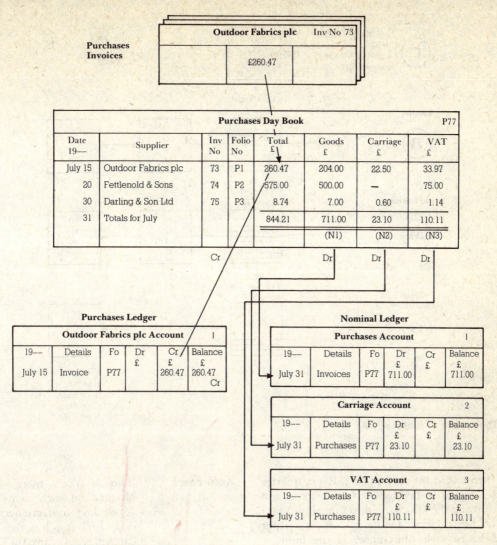

Fig 11   Procedure for dealing with purchases invoices

Purchases Day Book (Fig 11). It will be seen that both the invoice numbers and the folio numbers are entered in this book. Folio numbers relate to the pages of the accounts where the entries have been posted. The amount of the invoice appears twice: once as a total, and again analysed according to the net amount of the goods, the carriage and VAT. The total value of the goods is entered in the debit column of the purchases account and the VAT charge appears in the debit column of the VAT account in the Nominal Ledger. The Purchases Ledger contains the personal accounts of all the firm's suppliers (creditors), whereas the Nominal Ledger contains the impersonal accounts such as purchases, carriage and VAT. Examples of these accounts are given in Fig 11.

3.3 Value added tax

Value added tax is a charge on the supply of certain goods and services made in the United Kingdom by a person or firm registered for VAT. Whenever a trader buys goods or services to which VAT applies, he receives from the supplier a tax invoice indicating the cost of the goods and the VAT charge on them. When, in turn, the trader supplies taxable goods and services to his customers he

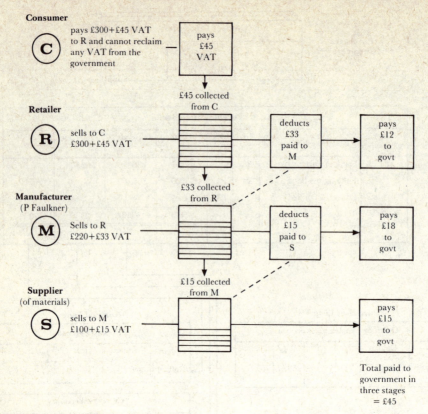

Consumer

C

pays £300+£45 VAT
to R and cannot reclaim
any VAT from the
government

pays
£45
VAT

£45 collected
from C

Retailer

R

sells to C
£300+£45 VAT

deducts
£33
paid to
M

pays
£12
to
govt

£33 collected
from R

Manufacturer
(P Faulkner)

M

Sells to R
£220+£33 VAT

deducts
£15
paid to
S

pays
£18
to
govt

£15 collected
from M

Supplier
(of materials)

S

sells to M
£100+£15 VAT

pays
£15
to
govt

Total paid to
government in
three stages
= £45

Fig 12 The process of collecting VAT

charges them tax at the current rate. Every quarter the trader makes a tax return to Customs and Excise, showing the tax charged to him (input tax) and the tax he has charged to his customers (output tax) and he pays the difference. If the input is greater than the output tax he is entitled to claim a refund of the difference. It will be seen that in the invoice on p 11 Faulkners are being charged £33.97 for VAT, representing 15% of the net invoice price of £226.50. They will add VAT to their invoices when they sell goods (see the sales invoice on p 47). In this capacity Faulkners are serving as a VAT collector on behalf of the government. The principle is illustrated in Fig 12 where Faulkners (M) receive materials from a supplier (S), manufacture and sell the finished articles to a retailer (R) who sells them to the consumer (C).

There are three categories of supply relating to VAT:

Standard rate: This is a percentage rate of tax, currently 15%, which is added to the value of supplies.

Zero rate: This is where there is no tax charged on such items as food (excluding confectionery), domestic fuel etc, but the business can still recover any VAT charged to it.

Exempt: This applies to certain services (eg insurance and postage) and land, which cannot charge VAT but still require to pay VAT on their purchases.

Further details concerning the calculation of VAT are given on p 54.

It is impracticable in business to pay for goods as they are received so it is customary for suppliers to give a reasonable time in which to pay, that is they allow credit and are, therefore, known as creditors; in other words they are the people to whom money is owing.

A fundamental rule when entering in the ledger is that the *giver* of either goods or money is *credited* and the *receiver* is *debited*. There are two effects to every transaction – receiving and giving – and for

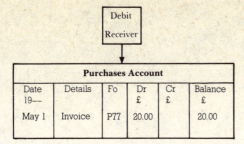

| Debit | Receiver |

| Credit | Giver |

Purchases Account

Date 19--	Details	Fo	Dr £	Cr £	Balance £
May 1	Invoice	P77	20.00		20.00

Supplier's Account

Date 19--	Details	Fo	Dr £	Cr £	Balance £
May 1	Invoice	P77		20.00	20.00 Cr

every receiver there must be a giver. In the example above the firm *receives* goods which it has purchased and the Purchases Account is debited. The supplier has *given* the goods to the firm and his account is, therefore, credited.

Both effects are always recorded in the ledger and this is known as the principle of double entry. It is essential for a business to have a record of its financial position as it affects receiving and giving, for example it wants to know what it owes each creditor as well as the value of the goods received from these creditors.

Guidelines for entering in ledger accounts

1 Accounts provide a permanent record and all entries should, therefore, be made with a pen.
2 Neatness is essential and lines should be drawn with a ruler.
3 The year must appear at the top of every date column.
4 It is usual to write the month followed by the date, eg Sept 19. Dittos can be used for repeating the month, but it is advisable to write the date in every time.
5 The details column contains a brief description of the nature of the transaction, eg invoice, payment, etc.
6 The folio column is used for recording the number of the page on which the original entry appears, eg P77, providing a quick and easy reference to the full information about the transaction and indicating that it has been entered in both places.
7 The balance column is updated after every entry, the purchase made on Sept 19 being indicated as a credit balance of £83.05. A further purchase, say of £50.00, would have the effect of increasing the credit balance to £133.05.

The format for setting out ledger accounts above, which is adopted throughout this book, is the normal practice in business. An alternative method, commonly used for hand-written accounts and known as the 'T' format, is as follows:

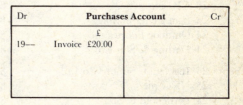

Dr	**Purchases Account**		Cr
19--	£ Invoice £20.00		

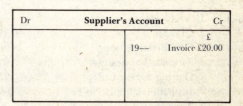

Dr	**Supplier's Account**		Cr
		19--	£ Invoice £20.00

The left side contains the debit entries (abbreviated Dr) and the right side the credit entries (abbreviated Cr). The difference between the two sides of an account is the balance. The Purchases Account in the above example has a debit balance because the debit side exceeds the credit side and the Supplier's Account has a credit balance as the credit side exceeds the debit side.

Exercises

Note: One set of accounts may be used for Exercises **1–3**, but if desired they can be treated separately.

Enter the following invoices in the Purchases Day Book, post them to the appropriate ledger accounts, total the Purchases Day Book at the end of each week and transfer the totals to the appropriate accounts in the Nominal Ledger.

	Date	Supplier	Invoice No	Total	Goods	Carriage	VAT
				£	£	£	£
1	Sept	19 NKG plc	80	831.45	703.00	20.00	108.45
		19 Tape Works Ltd	81	36.80	30.00	2.00	4.80
		20 Fettlenold & Sons	82	161.00	140.00	—	21.00
		20 CIC plc	83	483.00	400.00	20.00	63.00
		23 Sam Beller & Sons	84	40.25	33.00	2.00	5.25
		24 Outdoor Fabrics plc	85	86.82	68.00	7.50	11.32
		24 Darling & Son Ltd	86	89.70	73.00	5.00	11.70
2	Sept	25 Insulation Supply Co Ltd	87	49.45	43.00	—	6.45
		25 NKG plc	88	595.70	503.00	15.00	77.70
		25 Fettlenold & Sons	89	198.95	173.00	—	25.95
		26 CIC plc	90	368.80	307.20	13.50	48.10
		27 Outdoor Fabrics plc	91	103.50	82.10	7.90	13.50
		30 Darling & Son Ltd	92	82.22	67.00	4.50	10.72
		30 Insulation Supply Co Ltd	93	60.95	53.00	—	7.95
3	Oct	1 NKG plc	94	83.26	69.10	3.30	10.86
		1 CIC plc	95	304.17	253.20	11.30	39.67
		2 Sam Beller & Sons	96	30.26	25.00	1.32	3.94
		3 Outdoor Fabrics plc	97	59.54	47.32	4.45	7.77
		7 Darling & Son Ltd	98	126.20	102.00	7.75	16.45
		7 Insulation Supply Co Ltd	99	45.42	39.50	—	5.92
		7 Tape Works Ltd	100	27.83	23.17	1.03	3.63
4	Jan	2 B Draper & Sons plc	1	77.28	67.20	—	10.08
		3 Maytree Supply Co	2	489.09	403.10	22.20	63.79
		3 Godfrey & Fry Ltd	3	155.51	127.90	7.33	20.28
		3 Elliot Bros Ltd	4	235.98	193.16	12.04	30.78
		5 Derby Supply plc	5	92.57	76.37	4.13	12.07
		5 C Bond Ltd	6	233.68	203.20	—	30.48
		5 Sam Brown	7	23.17	23.17	—	—

```
                              CREDIT NOTE

                                                    No 776

              OUTDOOR FABRICS plc, Manchester Road, Bolton, Lancs BN3 2BT

   Tel: 0204 22016
   VAT Registration No: 199 0188 25
                                          Date:  28 July 19—
                                          Ref: Invoice No  437
                                             dated      15/7/–

   To:      P Faulkner & Sons           Original supply: Sale
            Chestnut Avenue
            Southampton
            SO2 4AG
```

Quantity	Details	Price £	Cost £	VAT rate %	VAT amount £
	Allowance for defective part of delivery TC 743 G		30.00		
	Less trade discount 15%		4.50		
			25.50	15	3.82
	Plus VAT		3.82		
			29.32		

```
   Goods received  ⎫
   Price/Terms     ⎬  JW
   Extensions      ⎭
   C/N No              17
   PRB Folio           PR 13
```

Fig 13   A credit note (usually printed in red)

3.4 Purchases returns

One of the consignments in the Goods Received Section had been reported, at a later stage, to be defective. The defect was reported to the buyer, who had contacted the supplier to negotiate an acceptable allowance. The supplier, Outdoor Fabrics plc, agreed to allow £30 off the list price and they sent the credit note (Fig 13) to P Faulkner & Sons.

Trade discount is deducted, as on the original invoice, because the allowance was given off the list price. In addition, the VAT charge must also be added to the amount of the allowance.

A credit note is a document sent by a supplier to his customer when the amount originally charged on an invoice is too much, ie it is a reduction of the amount of the invoice, thus forming a correction.

The accounts provide a permanent record of transactions and once an entry has been made it can be amended only by making a further entry. An entry must not be crossed out nor, even worse, erased. The principal reasons for issuing credit notes are to provide for:

a an allowance for goods damaged in transit or found to be defective on arrival
b a return of goods by the customer to the supplier
c an adjustment for short delivery
d correction of an overcharge arising from an error in the arithmetic, ie price, quantity or extensions
e an allowance for returnable cases, jars, etc

All of these allowances are described as purchases returns although some of them do not entail the actual returning of goods. Whatever the reason the

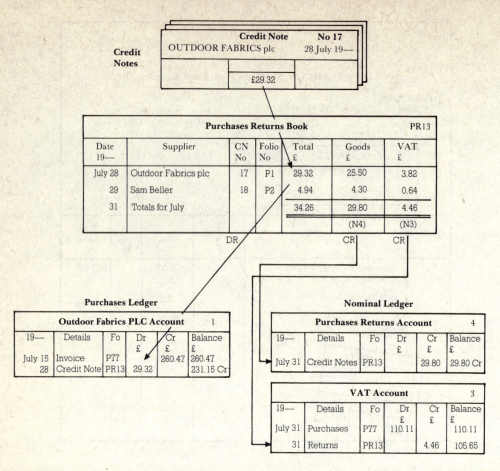

Fig 14   Procedure for dealing with suppliers' credit notes

procedure is the same, ie the supplier issues a credit note which is:

a checked
b allocated a number for reference purposes and filing
c entered in a Purchases Returns Book
d posted to the ledger accounts – the customers' accounts are debited because it is a cancellation of part of a purchase which had been credited. The total of the value of the goods is credited to a purchases returns account whilst the VAT is credited to the VAT Account.

When a credit note is received it has to be checked with the discrepancy noted on the goods received note or a report made at a later stage and the information supplied in the invoice. The initials of

the checker and the reference numbers of the Purchases Returns Book are inserted in the spaces provided on the rubber-stamp impression on the credit note.

Exercises

1   Enter the credit notes on pp 21 and 22 in the Purchases Returns Book, post them to the appropriate ledger accounts, total the Purchases Returns Book at the end of the month and transfer the totals to the appropriate accounts in the Nominal Ledger.

CREDIT NOTE

No 419

DARLING & SON, Mawney Road, Romford, Essex RD7 2OP

VAT Registration No 290 0943 20

Date: 3 October 19--
Ref: Invoice No 743
dated 24/9/--

Original Supply: Sale

To:
P Faulkner & Sons
Chestnut Avenue
Southampton
SO2 4AG

Quantity	Details	Price £	Amount £	VAT rate %	VAT amount £
12	Tent zips faulty (unserviceable)	70p	8.40	15	1.26
	Plus VAT		1.26		
			9.66		

Goods received	JW
Price/Terms	
Extensions	19
C/N No	
PRB Folio	

CREDIT NOTE

No 120

TAPE WORKS LIMITED, Nettle Lane, Nottingham NM1 8OR

VAT Registration No 156 0785 53

Date: 10 October 19--
Ref: Invoice No 437
dated 7/10/--

Original Supply: Sale

To:
P Faulkner & Sons
Chestnut Avenue
Southampton
SO2 4AG

Quantity	Description	Price each £	Amount £	VAT rate %	VAT amount £
2 bobbins	Short delivery of 5 m/m brown webbing	£3.60 per bobbin	7.20	15	1.08
	Plus VAT		1.08		
			8.28		

Goods received	JW
Price/Terms	
Extensions	20
C/N No	
PRB Folio	

CREDIT NOTE

No 473

CIC plc, Lanchester, Co Durham DM4 9SA

VAT Registration No 283 0568 20

Date: 23 October 19—
Ref: Invoice No 274
    dated   1/10/—

To:

P Faulkner & Sons
Chestnut Avenue
Southampton
SO2 4AG

Original supply: Sale

Quantity	Description	Price each £	Cost £	VAT rate %	VAT amount £
150 metres	Nylon reinforced PVC returned – substandard	£1.40 per metre	210.00		
	Less trade discount 15%		31.50		
			178.50		
	Plus VAT		26.77	15	26.77
			205.27		

Goods received	
Prices/Terms	JW
Extensions	
C/N No	21
PRB Folio	

2 *a* What information can be gained from the two documents shown below?

b Assuming that there are no other entries, write up the account of R B Bee in M Menton's ledger.

```
┌────────────────────────────────────────────────────────────────┐
│                    INVOICE                    No 727            │
│                                                                  │
│        Dr to                R  B  BEE                            │
│                                                                  │
│                                              Old Lane            │
│                                              Exton               │
│                                                                  │
│                                              8/6/19–              │
│        M Menton                                                  │
│        Lecham                                                    │
│        Order No 41                                               │
│                                                                  │
│                                                 £                │
│            6    Type 49 metal fittings  £12 ea   72.00           │
│            6    Type 51 metal fittings  £ 6 ea   36.00           │
│                                                108.00            │
│                                                ══════            │
│                                                                  │
└────────────────────────────────────────────────────────────────┘
```

```
┌────────────────────────────────────────────────────────────────┐
│        Cr by                                                     │
│                             R  B  BEE                            │
│                                                                  │
│                                              Old Lane            │
│                                              Exton               │
│                                                                  │
│                                              14/6/19––            │
│        M Menton                                                  │
│        Lecham                                                    │
│                                                                  │
│            3 Type 49 metal fittings    £12 ea    £36.00          │
│            returned faulty                                       │
│                                                                  │
└────────────────────────────────────────────────────────────────┘
```

3 Enter the following documents in the appropriate day books, post them to the ledger accounts, total the books at the end of the month and transfer the totals to the respective accounts in the Nominal Ledger. Allocate appropriate reference numbers for the documents and books.

Date		Supplier	Document	Goods	Carriage	VAT
				£	£	£
May	1	Darling & Son Ltd	Invoice	80.00	5.00	12.75
	4	CIC plc	Invoice	105.00	8.00	16.95
	8	Darling & Son Ltd	Credit note	8.00	—	1.20
	10	Insulation Supply Co Ltd	Invoice	25.00	3.00	4.20
	12	CIC plc	Credit note	5.00	—	0.75

```
                        STATEMENT
                    OUTDOOR FABRICS PLC
                       Manchester Road,
                     Bolton, Lancs BN3 2BT
                    Telephone: Bolton 22016

Tel: 0204 22016


To:    ┌─────────────────────────────┐
       │ P Faulkner & Sons           │
       │ Chestnut Avenue             │
       │ Southampton                 │
       │ SO2 4AG                     │         Date: 31 July 19—
       └─────────────────────────────┘


Terms:  Net payment within one month
```

Date	Details	Ref No	Dr £	Cr £	Balance £
19—					
July 15	Invoice	437	260.47		260.47
28	Credit note	776		29.32	231.15

The last amount in the balance column is the amount owing
Please return this statement with your remittance.

Fig 15   Statement

3.5 Payment for purchases and reconciliation of statements with ledger accounts

Once a month the suppliers send out statements of account to their customers in order to remind them of the amounts due to be paid. A statement of account is a copy of a customer's account in the ledger and it can be used by the customer to check the entries made in his Purchases Ledger before making payment. The statement which Outdoor Fabrics plc would send P Faulkner & Sons at the end of September is shown in Fig 15. It will be seen that the statement agrees with the Purchases Ledger Account of Outdoor Fabrics plc (p 20) but it is debited, whereas in Faulkner's accounts it is credited. This transaction in Outdoor Fabrics' accounts is a sale which is debited because Faulkners received the goods. On the other hand, the transaction appears as a purchase in Faulkner's accounts, and Outdoor Fabrics' account is credited to show that they were the givers. The ledger accounts in the two firms would be as shown on p 25.

If the statement is correct it is initialled and passed to the Cashier's Section for payment.

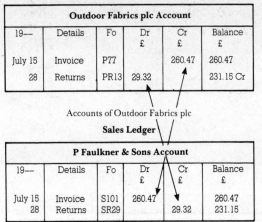

Accounts of P Faulkner & Sons

Purchases Ledger

Outdoor Fabrics plc Account

19—	Details	Fo	Dr £	Cr £	Balance £
July 15	Invoice	P77		260.47	260.47
28	Returns	PR13	29.32		231.15 Cr

Accounts of Outdoor Fabrics plc

Sales Ledger

P Faulkner & Sons Account

19—	Details	Fo	Dr £	Cr £	Balance £
July 15	Invoice	S101	260.47		260.47
28	Returns	SR29		29.32	231.15

On some occasions the statement, at first sight, may not agree with the ledger account. For example, the statement below from Fettlenold & Sons shows a balance of £670.98 owing by Faulkners, whereas Fettlenold's ledger account shows the balance as £550.00. Each item on the statement has to be checked with the corresponding entry in the ledger and any omissions or errors are entered in a reconciliation statement (see p 26). In this case the difference between the statement and the ledger account is made up (or reconciled) by deducting the payment made on 30 July from the statement balance. At the time of despatching the statement Fettlenold & Sons had not received the payment and could not, therefore, include it in the statement. The accounts clerk at Faulkners would have to deduct the payment made on 30 July from the statement before passing it for payment.

STATEMENT

FETTLENOLD & SONS
Birch Lane, Birmingham B29 2BR

Tel: 021 493 6892

To: P Faulkner & Sons
Chestnut Avenue
Southampton
SO2 4AG

Date: 31 July 19—

Terms: Payment due in 30 days

Date	Details	Ref No	Dr £	Cr £	Balance £
19—					
July 1	Balance				120.98
20	Invoice	321	575.00		695.98
27	Returns	33		25.00	670.98

Payment of the balance within the time stated will be appreciated

Accounts of P Faulkner & Sons
Purchases Ledger

Fettlenold & Sons Account

19—	Details	Fo	Dr £	Cr £	Balance £
June 20	Invoice	64		120.98	120.98
July 20	Invoice	74		575.00	695.98
27	Returns	26	25.00		670.98
30	Payment		120.98		550.00 Cr

Reconciliation statement
for Fettlenold & Sons' Account

	£
Balance as per statement (31/7/19—)	670.98
Deduct payment made on 30/7/19—	120.98
Balance as per ledger account	550.00

Reconciliation statement

A difference arose in connection with the statement received from Darling & Son Ltd:

STATEMENT

DARLING & SON LTD
Mawney Road, Romford, Essex RD7 2OP

Tel: 0708 416938

To:

P Faulkner & Sons
Chestnut Avenue,
Southampton SO2 4AG

Date: 30 July 19—

Date	Details	Ref No	Dr £	Cr £	Balance £
19—					
July 1	Balance				20.00
30	Invoice	432	9.84		29.84

Please remit the balance within one month

In the ledger of P Faulkner & Sons, Darling & Son Ltd's Account shows:

19—	Details	Fo	Dr £	Cr £	Balance £
June 28	Invoice	68		25.66	25.66
30	Returns	27	5.66		20.00
30	Invoice	75		8.94	28.94 Cr

It is clear that the £0.90 difference arises from a transposition of figures; the amount of £8.94 was found to be correct and the excess of £0.90 was deducted from the statement, reconciling it with the ledger account before passing it for payment. The reconciliation statement is as follows:

Reconciliation Statement
for Darling & Son Ltd Account

	£
Balance as per statement (30/7/19—)	29.84
Deduct amount for incorrect invoice entry on 30 July 19—	0.90
Balance as per ledger account	28.94

Instructions for the preparation of cheques

1 Always use a pen for writing cheques.
2 After 'Pay' write the correct name of the payee (ie the name of the person to whom the cheque is made payable).
3 Insert the amount in words as well as in figures, except for the pence which are shown in figures only.
4 Do not leave spaces for other words or figures to be added.
5 The day, month and year must be given in the date.
6 A record of the date, the payee's name and the amount should be entered on the counterfoil.
7 All cheques should be crossed before being sent through the post to ensure that they are paid into a bank account.
8 Cheques are signed by Mr P Faulkner, as well as by Mr S Faulkner, the Chief Accountant.

The following cheque (Fig 16) was made out to Outdoor Fabrics plc for the amount outstanding in their account:

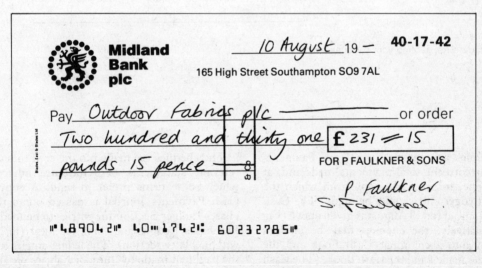

Fig 16 A cheque

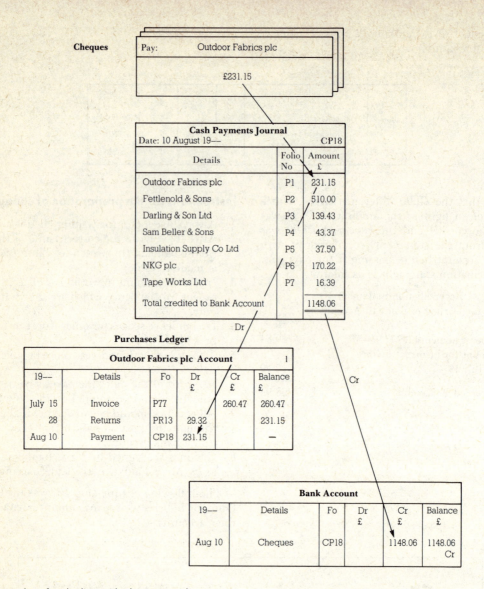

Cheques

Pay:	Outdoor Fabrics plc
	£231.15

Cash Payments Journal
Date: 10 August 19—   CP18

Details	Folio No	Amount £
Outdoor Fabrics plc	P1	231.15
Fettlenold & Sons	P2	510.00
Darling & Son Ltd	P3	139.43
Sam Beller & Sons	P4	43.37
Insulation Supply Co Ltd	P5	37.50
NKG plc	P6	170.22
Tape Works Ltd	P7	16.39
Total credited to Bank Account		1148.06

Dr

Purchases Ledger

Outdoor Fabrics plc Account   1

19—	Details	Fo	Dr £	Cr £	Balance £
July 15	Invoice	P77		260.47	260.47
28	Returns	PR13	29.32		231.15
Aug 10	Payment	CP18	231.15		—

Cr

Bank Account

19—	Details	Fo	Dr £	Cr £	Balance £
Aug 10	Cheques	CP18		1148.06	1148.06 Cr

Fig 17   Procedure for dealing with cheques paid

The cheques are entered in a Cash Payments Journal to record the total payments made and, at the same time, to provide a copy from which the Purchases Ledger entries may be made. The Cash Payments Journal for 10 August is given above (Fig 17). Alternatively, the cheques may be entered individually into a columnar Cash Book and the ledger entries made from the Cash Book. (The Cash book is dealt with in detail in Section 6.1, p 71.)

The cheques are mailed to the creditors with the relevant statements or remittance advice notes which some firms prefer to send. A copy of the Cash Payments Journal is passed on to the Purchases Ledger Section for entries to be made in the Purchases Ledger and Bank Account (to be dealt with in a later section). The ledger entries to record the payment made to Outdoor Fabrics plc are given in the procedure for dealing with cheques paid.

Midland Bank plc

bank giro credit
summary form

Branch _____ Southampton _____ Date __ 25.2.19—

Please distribute the bank giro credits attached as arranged with the recipients.

Our cheque for £ __ 613.34 __ is enclosed.

Number of Items
7

Customer _____ P FAULKNER & SONS

Address _____ Chestnut Avenue
Southampton SO2 4AG

Signature/s _____ S Faulkner

Bank sorting code number	For account of and account number		Amount		Total amount for each bank	
30.00.09	NKG Limited	23451834	28	14		
30-19-62	Tape Works Limited	81093263	119	00		
30-84-31	Fettlenold & Sons	62345582	18	60		
					165	74
40-17-38	CIC plc	34649810	104	23		
40-23-61	Sam Beller & Sons	23418776	52	00		
					156	23
20-14-32	Outdoor Fabrics plc	12300987	231	15		
20-89-66	Darling & Son Ltd	78452960	60	22		
					291	37
	Totals carried forward £		613	34	613	34

Fig 18 Bank Giro credits

Note that the payment is *debited* to record the fact that Outdoor Fabrics plc *receive* the amount and that the account has been settled, resulting in a nil balance.

Alternative methods of payment such as credit transfers or National Giro might be used for settling accounts.

Credit transfer (or Bank Giro) is a bank service which enables a firm to pay its creditors without having to prepare separate cheques for each account. A list (Fig 18) is sent to the bank periodically, with credit slips and a cheque for the total amount. The bank then arrange for the credit slips to be sent to the creditors through their branches.

The Post Office provides a similar credit transfer facility using the National Giro system, the list (or schedule) of payments being sent by post to the Giro Centre.

Exercises

1 *a* Prepare the personal accounts in the Purchases Ledger of P Faulkner & Sons as you would expect them to appear from the information supplied in the statements sent by the suppliers listed below.

b Prepare cheques dated 10 November to settle the accounts for these suppliers, list the items in a Cash Payments Journal and post them to the personal accounts in the Purchases Ledger.

Darling & Son Ltd

Date 19—	Details	Ref No	Dr £	Cr £	Balance £
Oct 7	Invoice	174	123.74		123.74
14	Invoice	203	203.13		326.87
16	Returns	43		23.10	303.77

Insulation Supply Co Ltd

Date 19—	Details	Ref No	Dr £	Cr £	Balance £
Oct 7	Invoice	1329	43.00		43.00
23	Invoice	1374	110.23		153.23
30	Returns	76		17.10	136.13

C I C plc

Date 19—	Details	Ref No	Dr £	Cr £	Balance £
Oct 1	Brought forward				76.92*
10	Payment			76.92	–
11	Invoice	7624X	137.23		137.23
16	Returns	431		137.23	–
18	Invoice	7726X	116.27		116.27
23	Invoice	7829X			256.52
27	Returns	434		14.03	242.49

* Note this is the amount which was due for a transaction in September.

2 Study the statement below and state:

a the name of the person supplying the goods

b the significance of the three columns numbered **1, 2** and **3**

c the names of the debtor and creditor and the amount owed on 31 May 19—. (*RSA BKI*)

Statement

In account with

T Wilkinson and Company Ltd
12 Hull Rd
Bridlington B3

31 May 19—

J W Joyce
14 Moor St
Bilston

		1 £	2 £	3 £
May 1	Balance			120.98
7	Invoice 254	120.14		241.12
8	Cheque		117.37	
	Discount		3.61	120.14
8	Invoice 297	78.10		198.24
10	Returns		15.24	183.00
15	Credit note			
	Overcharge		2.50	180.50
25	Invoice 509	147.00		327.50

---

3 Enter the documents below in the appropriate day books, post them to the ledger accounts, total the books at the end of the month and transfer the totals to the respective accounts in the nominal ledger and the Bank Account. Allocate appropriate reference numbers for the documents and books.

Date	Supplier	Document	Goods £	Carriage £	VAT £
Nov 1	Fettlenold & Sons	Invoice	105.00	15.00	18.00
5	Sam Beller & Sons	Invoice	14.00	1.00	2.25
8	Tape Works Ltd	Invoice	240.00	—	36.00
12	Sam Beller & Sons	Credit note	4.00	—	0.60
26	Fettlenold & Sons	Invoice	84.00	6.00	13.50
30	Fettlenold & Sons Sam Beller & Sons Tape Works Ltd	Cheques sent to settle their accounts			

4 Check the following statement received from Southampton Welding Co with the account in Faulkners Purchases Ledger and prepare a statement to reconcile the balances.

STATEMENT

SOUTHAMPTON WELDING CO
Millbrook Industrial Estate, Southampton SO4 3AL

Tel: 0703 492231

To: P Faulkner & Sons
Chestnut Avenue
Southampton
SO2 4AG

Date: 15 January 19—

Terms: Payment due in 30 days

Date	Details	Ref No	Dr £	Cr £	Balance £
19—					
Jan 1	Balance				53.00
6	Invoice	A1162	37.62		90.62
12	Returns	416		2.33	88.29

The last amount in the balance column is the amount owing

Accounts of P Faulkner & Sons

Purchases Ledger

Southampton Welding Co Account					
19—	Details	Fo	Dr £	Cr £	Balance £
Jan 1	Balance				53.00
6	Invoice	431		27.62	80.62
12	Returns	26	2.33		78.29
30	Payment		53.00		25.29

3.6 Simultaneous records

The work involved in making out cheques, entering them in the Cash Payments Journal and posting the payments to the suppliers' accounts involves using the same figures three times. Similarly, the work involved with purchases invoices and statements causes the supplier to enter the invoices in the Sales Day Book, post them to the customers' accounts in the Sales Ledger and eventually prepare statements. This work can be carried out more efficiently by using simultaneous records and avoiding the possibility of transferring wrong figures (quite a common error in ordinary manual systems). The answer lies in using a copywriter board, sometimes referred to as a manifold bill board, or a three-in-one system which produces simultaneous records.

The simultaneous record procedure for purchases is as follows:

1 The invoices are sorted into the order required, either numerically by account number or alphabetically by suppliers' names.
2 A print calculator is used to add up:
   a the net value of the goods;
   b the value of the VAT charged;
   c the net value of the invoices or the total of *a* and *b*.
   This operation is called pre-listing.
3 A proof sheet is placed on the copywriter board (this takes the place of the Purchases Day Book).
4 A sheet of carbon paper is placed over the proof sheet, or NCR paper (no carbon required) is used.
5 The supplier's ledger account is selected for the first invoice, lined up with the proof sheet and placed on top of the carbon paper. Care must be taken to ensure that the last line entered in the ledger account lines up with the last entry made in the proof sheet so that the new entry appears on the next available line in both records. The ledger sheets may be housed in a posting tray for convenient selection and extraction of sheets.
6 The old balance, as provided on the ledger sheet, is entered and the supplier's name written on the proof sheet only. The amount of the invoice is credited and the new balance updated with the addition of the new item. The VAT and the goods figures can be shown separately on the ledger sheet, but it is not essential. By providing these separate figures

and totals on the proof sheet an additional check is provided with the pre-list which is useful for VAT purposes.
7 The supplier's account sheet is removed from the board, and the next supplier's ledger account selected for updating. The work proceeds in the manner described above, but care has to be taken to place the second supplier's account sheet on the line of the proof sheet immediately below the first entry.
8 When all the invoices have been posted, the columns on the proof sheet are totalled and it will be seen that:

$$\text{Total of old balances} + \text{Total of credit entries} = \text{Total of new balances}$$

also

$$\text{Total of credit entries} = \text{Total of pre-list (Goods + VAT)}$$

providing a conclusive check on the arithmetical accuracy of the work carried out.
9 The totals of the pre-list, as confirmed by the totals on the proof sheet, are posted to the Nominal Ledger as follows:

   a Net value of goods → debit → Purchases Account

   b VAT → debit → VAT Account

   c Net value of invoices → credit → Purchases Ledger Control Account (to be explained on p 38)

10 When the suppliers are paid the cheques are entered in a Cash Payments Journal which is posted to the ledger accounts as follows:

   a Individual cheques → debit → Supplier's Account

   b Total amount of cheques → credit → Bank Account

   c Total amount of cheques → debit → Purchases Ledger Control Account

The Cash Payments Journal and cheque-writing are entered simultaneously on a copywriter board.

11 The procedure for dealing with credit notes received is as follows:

    a The credit notes are pre-listed, providing totals for:

        i the net value of the goods

        ii the VAT charges and

        iii the net value of the credit notes, which equals the combined totals of *i* and *ii*.

    b The credit notes are debited to the suppliers' ledger accounts.

    c The totals of the pre-list are posted to the nominal ledger as follows:

        i The net value of →credit →Purchases the goods Returns Account

        ii VAT →credit →VAT Account

        iii The net value of →debit →Purchases the credit notes Ledger Control Account

The advantages of keeping simultaneous records are:

1 A check is provided on the accuracy of the postings and the balance calculations.

2 Entries are made simultaneously, avoiding the possibility of transposition errors and saving clerical time.

3 Work peaks are avoided at the end of the month, for example when entering sales transactions the statements are prepared at the same time as the ledger entries and are ready for despatch immediately the last entry is made.

4 The equipment is not expensive and little training is required to operate the system.

The three-in-one system for purchases and purchases returns is illustrated in Fig 19 on p 34.

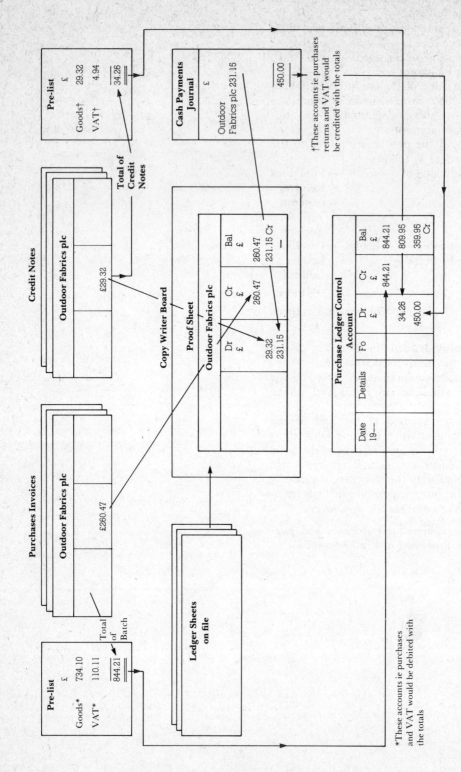

Fig 19 The three-in-one system for purchases and purchases returns

Exercises

1   Prepare Purchases Ledger Accounts, as on 1 January for the following six suppliers (addresses are given in the suppliers index on p 5) with the balances and account numbers supplied:

Supplier	Account No	Balance £
Sam Beller & Sons	101	70.00
CIC plc	102	—
Darling & Son Ltd	103	120.00
Insulation Supply Co Ltd	104	—
NKG plc	105	400.00
Outdoor Fabrics plc	106	—

Sort the following invoices into alphabetical order; pre-list the goods and VAT figures; add the two totals to find the total invoice batch.

Darling & Son Ltd		Insulation Supply Co Ltd		NKG plc	
4 Jan 19—	£	4 Jan 19—	£	7 Jan 19—	£
Goods	264.00	Goods	470.00	Goods	1312.50
VAT	39.60	VAT	70.50	VAT	196.87
	303.60		540.50		1509.37
Sam Beller & Sons		**CIC plc**		**Outdoor Fabrics plc**	
3 Jan 19—	£	3 Jan 19—	£	4 Jan 19—	£
Goods	225.00	Goods	1440.00	Goods	204.00
VAT	33.75	VAT	216.00	VAT	30.60
	258.75		1656.00		234.60

Number the invoices consecutively starting at number 734, then enter them into the accounts for the week ending 7 January using a system for simultaneous records. Check the totals on the proof sheet with the pre-list and if they are correct post them to the Nominal Ledger.

2 Using the same Purchases Ledger accounts as in Exercise **1** and following the same procedure enter the purchases invoices given below:

Date 19—	Supplier	Total value £	Goods £	VAT £	Invoice numbers
Week ending 14 January 19—					
Jan 10	Sam Beller & Sons	468.05	407.00	61.05	
11	Outdoor Fabrics plc	264.50	230.00	34.50	740
12	Darling & Son Ltd	137.42	119.50	17.92	to
12	NKG plc	667.00	580.00	87.00	745
14	Sam Beller & Sons	540.50	470.00	70.50	
14	Outdoor Fabrics plc	1 278.25	1 111.53	166.72	
Week ending 21 January 19—					
Jan 17	CIC plc	644.92	560.80	84.12	
18	Insulation Supply Co Ltd	1 176.56	1 023.10	153.46	746
19	Darling & Son Ltd	455.45	396.05	59.40	to
20	CIC plc	383.21	333.23	49.98	750
21	Insulation Supply Co Ltd	145.05	126.14	18.91	
Week ending 28 January 19—					
Jan 24	Sam Beller & Sons	230.00	200.00	30.00	
24	CIC plc	345.00	300.00	45.00	
24	Outdoor Fabrics plc	460.00	400.00	60.00	751
24	Darling & Son Ltd	908.50	790.00	118.50	to
25	NKG plc	1 115.50	970.00	145.50	757
26	Sam Beller & Sons	141.45	123.00	18.45	
27	NKG plc	151.80	132.00	19.80	

Enter the following credit notes received from the suppliers and debit their accounts:

Date 19—	Supplier	Total value £	Goods £	VAT £	Credit note No
Jan 12	CIC plc	23.00	20.00	3.00	43
19	NKG plc	17.25	15.00	2.25	44

Enter the following cheques into the Cash Payments Journal and debit the suppliers' ledger accounts:

		£
Jan 31	Sam Beller & Sons	70.00
31	Darling & Son Ltd	120.00
31	NKG plc	200.00

Check the totals on the proof sheets with the respective pre-lists and if they are correct post them to the nominal ledger.

3 Using the same Purchases Ledger accounts as in Exercises **1** and **2** and following the same procedure enter the purchases invoices given below:

Date 19—	Supplier	Total value £	Goods £	VAT £	Invoice numbers
Week ending 4 February 19—					
Feb 2	Sam Beller & Sons	287.50	250.00	37.50	758
3	Outdoor Fabrics plc	373.75	325.00	48.75	to
4	Darling & Son Ltd	479.55	417.00	62.55	760
Week ending 11 February 19—					
Feb 9	Insulation Supply Co Ltd	264.88	230.34	34.54	
9	NKG plc	1 956.15	1 701.00	255.15	761
10	CIC plc	931.50	810.00	121.50	to
11	NKG plc	1 398.12	1 215.76	182.36	765
11	CIC plc	1 024.07	890.50	133.57	
Week ending 18 February 19—					
Feb 16	Sam Beller & Sons	480.64	417.95	62.69	
16	CIC plc	1 390.81	1 209.40	181.41	766
17	Darling & Son Ltd	66.47	57.80	8.67	to
17	Insulation Supply Co Ltd	480.58	417.90	62.68	770
17	Sam Beller & Sons	644.41	560.36	84.05	
Week ending 25 February 19—					
Feb 23	Outdoor Fabrics plc	1 506.20	1 309.74	196.46	771
24	CIC plc	480.24	417.60	62.64	to
25	Darling & Son Ltd	96.60	84.00	12.60	774
25	Insulation Supply Co Ltd	598.69	520.60	78.09	

Enter the following credit notes received from the suppliers and debit their accounts:

Date 19—	Supplier	Total value £	Goods £	VAT £	Credit note No
Feb 14	Sam Beller & Sons	20.47	17.80	2.67	45
22	Darling & Son Ltd	11.50	10.00	1.50	46
25	CIC plc	6.90	6.00	0.90	47

Enter the following cheques into the Cash Payments Journal and debit the Suppliers' Ledger accounts:

		£
Feb 28	Sam Beller & Sons	1 638.75
28	CIC plc	3 006.13
28	Outdoor Fabrics plc	2 637.35
28	Darling & Son	1 804.97
28	Insulation Supply Co Ltd	1 862.11
28	NKG plc	3 226.42

Check the totals on the proof sheets with the respective pre-lists and if they are correct post them to the Nominal Ledger.

3.7 An introduction to Purchases Ledger Control Accounts

In addition to the accounts already described it is necessary to have a system of checking the accuracy of the ledgers by keeping a record of the totals in a separate account known as the Purchases Ledger Control Account. The relationship of the Control Account with the other accounting records is shown in Fig 19, p 34.

The Purchases Ledger Control Account is kept in the Nominal Ledger and represents a summary of all the items which have been posted to the Purchases Ledger, for example:

1 The credit balances of the creditors (opening balances).
2 *Add* purchases on credit.
3 *Deduct* purchases returns.
4 *Deduct* cheques paid and any cash discount (if it has been claimed see Unit 6.1, p 73).
5 Final balance = the balances of the creditors (closing balances).

The procedure for opening and keeping the Purchases Ledger Control Account, based on the figures in Section 3.6 (Exercises 1 and 2) on pp 35 and 36 is as follows:

1 Total the creditors' balances at the beginning of the month, ie £70 + £120 + £400 = £590 and enter the total as a credit balance on 1 January.
2 When the proof sheet (or Purchases Day Book) containing the purchases invoices has been cross-checked with the pre-list, the total of the net value of the invoices is credited to the Purchases Ledger Control Account and the balance updated, ie for the week ending 7 January the total is £4502.82. The totals of the purchases invoices for the successive weeks are credited to the Control Account.

3 The total of the credit notes, as entered in the Purchases Returns Book, is debited to the Control Account.
4 The total of the cheques paid, as listed in the cash payments journal, is debited to the Control Account.
5 The final balance, resulting from the above entries, should equal the total of all the creditors' accounts in the Purchases Ledger thus providing a check on the arithmetical accuracy of the ledger postings.

Exercises

1 Prepare the Purchases Ledger Control Account for February using the balance from the Purchases Ledger Control Account given above and the figures supplied in Exercise 3 of Section 3.6 (p 37).
2 Prepare a Purchases Ledger Control Account from the following details:

		£
April 1	Total of credit balances in Purchases Ledger	7 324.00
30	Purchases on credit for the month	2 322.00
30	Purchases returns for the month	206.00
30	Payments for the month	2 397.00
30	Cash discount received	200.00

3 The following transactions took place during the month of May. Construct a Purchases Ledger Control Account given that on 1 May the balances in the suppliers' accounts = £4 593 credit:

Purchases invoices received £	Credit notes received £
437.00	47.00
234.00	23.00
112.00	9.00
472.00	
57.00	*Cheques paid* £
93.00	372.00
12.00	134.00
116.00	461.00
	231.00
	666.00

Purchases Ledger Control Account				
Date 19—	Details	Dr £	Cr £	Balance £
January 1	Balance			590.00
7	Purchases		4502.82	5092.82
14	Purchases		3355.72	8448.54
21	Purchases		2805.19	11253.73
28	Purchases		3352.25	14605.98
31	Purchase Returns	40.25		14565.73
31	Payments	390.00		14175.73 Cr

4 Sales

4.1 Sales promotion

No matter how well a business manufactures and designs its products no profit is made until a sale is satisfactorily concluded. It is, therefore, vitally important for a manufacturer to pay attention to the promotion of sales, as well as market research to find out what the consumer needs and is willing to pay for.

Faulkners exhibit their range of products at exhibitions in various parts of the country and sometimes abroad. The Advertising Section of the Sales Department regularly advertise in *Camping and Caravaning* and other journals for retailers in the trade; the national newspapers also carry the firm's advertisements for mail-order business. Sales representatives are employed in different parts of the country to call on established distributors and stimulate an interest in the firm's products. Catalogues and price lists are prepared by the Advertising Section for distribution to potential customers.

Faulkners issue a separate price list (Fig 20) and reference will need to be made to this in some of the transactions which follow.

Any customers requesting goods which require modifications and are not included in the normal range are supplied with **quotations**. A quotation may be sent in a letter or it may be a standard form such as Fig 21 on p 40.

It should be noted that the price and terms are offered for a stated period; it is used to specify a price for supplying goods or services. An **estimate** differs from a quotation in that the ultimate cost can vary from the 'estimated' price and it is usually supplied when work such as building or repairing has to be undertaken.

A potential customer will take into consideration a number of factors before deciding whether to accept a quotation. These may include:

a price
b quality of the goods
c delivery cost and time
d terms of payment, eg cash discount for payment within a prescribed period
e trade discount
f after-sales service and guarantee

P FAULKNER & SONS, Chestnut Avenue, Southampton SO2 4AG

Telephone: Southampton 7654321   Telex: FA 7812

19— Price List (excluding VAT)

	Cat No	£
Frame Tents		
Faulkner Major	734T	298.00
Faulkner Minor	754T	268.00
Faulkner Cadet	774T	238.00
Ridge Tents		
Faulkner Expedition	523T	157.00
Faulkner Ranger	553T	130.00
Faulkner Hiker	583T	112.00
Sleeping Bags (Terylene filled)		
Arctic 44	13SB	16.50
Temperate 38	14SB	14.25
Junior 36	15SB	13.10
Rucksacks		
Mount Farley (frame)	27R	22.50
Rover	29R	17.25
Guider	31R	15.10
Camp Beds		
Resteasy	79C	15.75
Sleepwell	81C	13.50

Terms: All prices include delivery anywhere on the United Kingdom mainland

Trade Discount: 10% on orders over £5000
15% on orders over £10000

Payment due one month after delivery
2½% cash discount for payment within 7 days of invoice

Fig 20   A price list

```
┌─────────────────────────────────────────────────────────────────────────┐
│                        QUOTATION                      No PC123            │
│                                                                           │
│                                                                           │
│                      P   FAULKNER & SONS                                  │
│                 Chestnut Avenue, Southampton    SO2 4AG                   │
│                                                                           │
│   Telephone:   0703 7654321                    Telex: FA 7812             │
│                                                                           │
│   Bankers: Midland Bank plc, Southampton                                  │
│   National Giro Account No 7/286/4321                                     │
│   ────────────────────────────────────────────────────────────────────  │
│                                                                           │
│                                              Date  1 May 19---            │
│                                                                           │
│                                                                           │
│   To:    Brentfords plc                                                   │
│          Weston House                                                     │
│          Piccadilly                                                       │
│          London W1V 9PA                                                   │
│                                                                           │
│   In reply to your enquiry dated 28 April 19--- we have pleasure in       │
│   quoting you for the following:                                          │
│                                                                           │
│       60 'Faulkner Major' frame tents in orange and gold supplied to      │
│       a modified size as per your drawing @ £260.00 each                  │
│       (offer valid for 3 months from this date)                           │
│                                                                           │
│                                                                           │
│   Terms:    Net cash within one month after delivery                      │
│             Price includes delivery costs but excludes VAT                │
│             Trade discount: 15%                                           │
│             Delivery: 2 months on receipt of order.                       │
│                                                                           │
│   We look forward to receiving your instructions which will receive our   │
│   prompt attention.                                                       │
│                                                                           │
│                                                                           │
│                                                                           │
│                                                                           │
│                                                    D Faulkner             │
│                                                    Sales Manager          │
└─────────────────────────────────────────────────────────────────────────┘
```

Fig 21   A quotation

Exercises

1 P Faulkner & Sons have received an inquiry from Messrs R Barber & Son, Tower House, Sale, Manchester, for supplying 20 Mount Farley rucksacks in orange (not offered from stock). These can be supplied at the special price of £23 each, excluding VAT, and with 10 per cent trade discount. Free delivery in one month. Terms of payment as per the standard price list. Quotation valid for 2 months.

Prepare the quotation which Faulkners would send to R Barber & Son in answer to this inquiry.

2 The firm you work for – Blackburn, Robson and Coates, of 29 Moor Road, Huddersfield – has received an inquiry from W Jessop, 178 Tufnell Street, Nottingham, about the following goods:

5/10 rolls men's suiting of good quality, in brown, grey and navy blue fine checks
6/8 rolls costume tweed in heather mixtures
10/12 rolls terylene and worsted suiting

All materials should be 1.5 m wide. Delivery required in good time for autumn trade.

Draft and complete the document that would be sent by your firm in answer to this inquiry, giving all the essential information. (*RSA OPI*)

3 *a* Write a reply to the letter below from Mr J R McIntosh and send him a quotation. Supply him with the answers to his questions and provide him with full details of the wine table, inventing prices, dimensions, date of delivery, etc.

b What is the difference between a quotation and an estimate? (*RSA OPII*)

---

141 Castle Road
Dundee
Scotland

11 November 19—

The Southern Trading Company
Frampton Road
Edgware   Middx

Dear Sirs

I was very interested to see an illustration of a wine table, in polished mahogany, in the October edition of 'The Squire' and I understand that you are the sole suppliers of this particular model.

Will you please send me full details of the wine table, including its price, size and the approximate date of delivery.

Yours faithfully

J R McIntosh

J R McIntosh

```
                        Order              No 1089

   From: Brentfords plc          To:  P Faulkner & Sons
         Weston House,                Chestnut Avenue
         Piccadilly,                  Southampton
         London W1V 9PA               SO2 4AG

         Telephone: 01-432 5819

                                Date: 8 May 19—

   Please supply:

   Sixty (60) 'Faulkner Major' frame tents
   as per your quotation Ref PC123 dated
   1 May 19—        @£260 each

   Deliver to: Our store at 149 High Street, Woking, Surrey


     Credit approval       mw
     Order checked         TB
     Confirmation of order TB       R Roberts
     Order entered         JR
                                    Buyer
```

Fig 22   An incoming order

4.2 Receipt of orders

When orders are received from customers they are
stamped with a rubber stamp to ensure that a set
procedure is followed. You will see the rubber-
stamp impression on the order form (Fig 22) which
was received from Brentfords plc in response to the
quotation sent to them.

The procedure for handling incoming orders,
controlled by the rubber-stamped impression, is as
follows:

1 Credit approval

When an order is received a check is carried out to
be reasonably sure that the customer will pay for
the goods on the due date. If a customer fails to
pay, this can result in a bad debt which is a serious
matter as the firm not only loses the profit but also
the cost of the goods and the VAT charged. The
first step to be taken when an order is received is to
refer to the records of customers to see if the firm
has dealt with the customer before. An extract from
these (A to D section), provided in a strip indexing
system, is given in Fig 23. If the firm has traded
with the customer before, as in the case of Brentfords plc the Sales Ledger will reveal if he was a
satisfactory payer; if not, then payment before
despatch of the order would probably be insisted
upon. Where a new customer is involved and the
order is above a predetermined amount (in Faulkner's case this is £500), a check is made on the
customer's creditworthiness. The procedure is to
ask the customer to supply credit references from
two traders who report on the customer's financial
stability. It may be established that a customer is
good for £500 but not for £2000, in which case the
credit is granted at the lower figure. If all is in order
the credit approval box on the order is initialled
and a new index strip is prepared for the records of
customers.

2 Order checked

When initialled this box indicates that the details
on the order have been checked to make sure that
they agree with the current price list and terms or
with a special quotation.

Name	Address	Account No	Credit limit £	Account balance at 1 January 19—	Area
Aldous N K & Sons	14 High Street, Winchester, Hants WR4 5QP	4872	3500		South
Andrews J G	129 Market Street, Bradford, West Yorks BD1 7AS	4001	3500		North
Arnold & Baker	The Headrow, Leeds, West Yorks LS8 4ST	3402	6000	70	North
Attwood Camping Distributors plc	48 Desborough Road, Eastleigh, Hants SO4 4AG	2340	4500		South
Bailey Brothers	School Lane, Littlemelton, Norwich, Norfolk NH8 1AD	1005	6000		Midlands
Baldwin Stores Ltd	Hipperholme, Halifax, West Yorks HX7 3MN	4004	6000	123	North
Bell & Sons	400 Princes Street, Edinburgh, Scotland EH3 9AS	3367	12000		North
Bostock (DIY)	4 High Street, Abingdon, Oxford OD4 2VC	4407	3500		South
Brentfords plc	Weston House, Piccadilly, London W1V 9PA	3660	20000		South
Brown & Co Ltd	140 Deansgate, Manchester MR3 1AT	1119	4000	74	North
Carters Sports	57 Victoria Street, Wolverhampton WN7 1DE	3030	5000	267	Midlands
Charles, Hugh	'Outdoor Centre', Shakespeare Street, Nottingham NM5 5AD	2323	3500		Midlands
Chudleigh & Sons	Edgbaston Shopping Arcade, Hagley Road, Birmingham BM6 8AK	1104	5000		Midlands
Clarke Brothers Ltd	40 Blandford Street, Sunderland, Durham SD8 4GF	4403	5000		North
Coleman, David (Sports Equipment) Ltd	Torrington, North Devon TN5 7BN	3344	10000	150	South
Credit I N & Co	Ruxley Corner, Sidcup, Kent SP9 4SD	1067	500	34	South
Davies Edna	2347 High Street, Swansea, S Wales SA6 4JH	3789	500	60	South
Dentford Donald	1 High Road, Wormley, Broxbourne, Herts BE3 8AS	4321	2000		South
Dreamland Ltd	8 Kings Road, Brentwood, Essex BD3 1TY	1009	6000		South
Dunn (Sports Outfitters) Ltd	25 Saville Row, London W1X 2AY	2244	15000	404	South

Fig 23   Strip indexing of customer records

3 Confirmation of order

All orders are confirmed as soon as possible after receipt, ie formally acknowledged and numbered, as in Fig 24 on p 44. This number is used for identification purposes on all correspondence relating to the order. The rubber-stamp procedure is used for all orders, whether they are received by letter or telephone, even if the order is for immediate collection from stock. Five copies of the confirmation order (or works order) are prepared for the following distribution:

1 The customer (in this case Brentfords plc).
2 Sales Department, to enter in the order book and file.

3 Works Department, to prepare the goods; or Stores Section if delivery is from stock.
4 Despatch Section, to prepare for delivery.
5 Costing Section, to check the costs.

Orders from customers are stapled behind the Sales Dept's file copy of the confirmation of order.

4 Order entered

An initial in this box on the order signifies that the order has been entered in the order book (Fig 25, p 44) so that its progress can be checked and to ensure that delivery is made on time.

Confirmation of Order

P FAULKNER & SONS
Chestnut Avenue
Southampton
SO2 4AG

Order No S63729
(Please quote in all correspondence)

Telephone: Southampton 7654321
Telex: FA 7812

To: Brentfords plc
Weston House,
Piccadilly,
London W1V 9PA

Date: 10 May 19—

We wish to confirm your order No 1089 Dated 8 May 19—

~~Telephoned~~

Quantity	Description	Cat No	Price
60	'Faulkner Major' frame tents as per our quotation PC123	734T	£260 each excluding VAT Delivered Woking

Terms: Net cash within one month after delivery
15% trade discount

Delivery: 8 July 19—
to your order at 149 High Street, Woking, Surrey

We accept no responsibility for delay in case of force majeure, strikes, lockouts or other circumstances beyond our control.

For P FAULKNER & SONS

Signed ...*D Faulkner*.............

Sales Manager

Fig 24   Confirmation of order form

Order Book

Date: 10 May 19—

Our Order No	Customer	Quantity	Cat No	Delivery	Comments	Delivered
S63720	Arnold & Baker	10	79C	8/7/19—	Send by BR	
S63721	Attwood Camping Distributors plc	6	754T	9/7/19—		
		6	774T	9/7/19—		
S63722	Bell & Sons	50	523T	10/7/19—	Send by van	
		40	553T	10/7/19—	Send by van	
S63723	Brown & Co Ltd	10	27R	8/7/19—		
S63724	Hugh Charles	8	79C	9/7/19—		
S63725	David Coleman (Sports Equipment) Ltd	10	523T)	8/7/19—		
		10	553T)			
S63726	Carters Sports	20	754T	7/7/19—		
S63727	Chudleigh & Sons	3	13SB	8/7/19—	To be collected	
S63728	I N Credit & Co	6	523T	10/7/19—		
S63729	Brentfords plc	60	734T	8/7/19—		

Fig 25   An order book

44 Introduction to Business Accounts

Advice/Despatch Note

P FAULKNER & SONS, Chestnut Avenue, Southampton SO2 4AG
Telephone: 0703 7654321   Telex: FA 7812

To: Brentfords plc   Reference: Order S63729
      Weston House,
      Piccadilly   Date: 6 July 19–
      London W1V 9PA

We wish to advise you that your order dated 8 May 19– has been
~~is ready to be~~ despatched

Quantity	Description	Cat No
60	'Faulkner Major' frame tents	734T

For P FAULKNER & SONS

J Jones

Fig 26 An advice/despatch note

When the order is made up it is transferred from the Works or Stores to the Despatch Section who have already received notification of it by the copy of the confirmation of order. At this stage the despatch clerk prepares an advice/despatch note (Fig 26) to inform the customer that the order has been despatched or is ready for despatch. A copy of the advice/despatch note is passed to the Sales Ledger Section of the Accounts Department so that they can prepare the invoice set (as explained in Section 5.1) and record the delivery in the order book.

Exercises

1 Prepare confirmations of orders for the following orders received today using your own reference numbers (the addresses are given in the records of customers on p 43 and the prices and terms are given in the price list on p 39).

N K Aldous & Sons
30 'Arctic 44' sleeping bags
20 'Temperate 38' sleeping bags
Prompt delivery (delivered two days after receipt of order)

Baldwin Stores Ltd
10 'Faulkner Expedition' ridge tents
15 'Faulkner Ranger' ridge tents
Delivery in one month

David Coleman (Sports Equipment) Ltd
30 'Mount Farley' rucksacks
20 'Rover' rucksacks
30 'Guider' rucksacks
40 'Faulkner Major' frame tents
30 'Faulkner Minor' frame tents
Delivery: rucksacks in one month
          Frame tents in two months

2 Enter the orders received in Exercise 1 into an order book.
3 Prepare an advice note for the goods ordered by N K Aldous & Sons in Exercise 1.
4 Every business which sells goods on credit wishes to avoid bad debts. Describe the steps which may be taken before a new customer is allowed credit.
    How may the customer be treated if his credit worthiness is a matter of doubt?   (*RSA BKI*)

5 Accounts – Sales Ledger Section

5.1 Sales invoices

The route of the copy advice/despatch note as it is processed by the Sales Ledger Section of the Accounts Department is now examined.

This section is much larger than the Purchases Ledger Section because the firm has to deal with about 3000 orders annually and prepare the same number of sales invoices (10 times as many as the Purchases Ledger Section). Although most of these are 'repeat orders' from the same customers, there are often as many as 200 accounts open at one time in the busy season from March to August. In order to spread the work out the sales ledger is divided into three sections, ie for customers A–D, E–L and M–Z. An extract of the customers' records at 1 January for the A–D section is given on p 43.

The sales invoices are prepared in 'sets' in one typing; alternatively, they can be prepared by accounting machine or computer. The diagram below shows how the 'set' is distributed.

The following procedure is adopted for preparing the sales invoice set:

1 The advice/despatch note is received from the Stores Section.
2 The copy order is extracted from the sales order file to obtain the prices and terms.
3 The sales invoice clerk calculates the prices on the invoice in readiness for typing.
4 Trade discount (referred to in the quotation and also in the price list) is deducted from the list price *before* VAT is calculated. The amount of VAT is calculated on the discounted value of the goods, including cash discount where appropriate. The discounted value is the price as given in the price list less any discounts. The rate and amount of VAT are shown in their respective columns against the items to which they refer. VAT is added to the net value of the goods to arrive at the net value of the invoice.

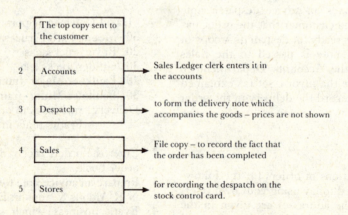

1	The top copy sent to the customer	
2	Accounts	→ Sales Ledger clerk enters it in the accounts
3	Despatch	→ to form the delivery note which accompanies the goods – prices are not shown
4	Sales	→ File copy – to record the fact that the order has been completed
5	Stores	→ for recording the despatch on the stock control card.

Additional copies may be required for representatives, statistics and market research.

```
                            INVOICE

                                                      No 1624

    From:  P FAULKNER & SONS, Chestnut Avenue, Southampton SO2 4AG


    Tel:    0703 7654321                   Telex:  FA 7812

    VAT Registration No  304 3739 11        Date: 8 July 19---

    To:   ┌─────────────────────────┐     Supply:  Sale
          │  Brentfords plc          │
          │  Weston House            │
          │  Piccadilly              │
          │  London W1V 9PA          │
          └─────────────────────────┘

    Terms:  Net cash within one month after delivery
            Delivered Woking

    Completion of Order No 1089    dated  8 May 19---
```

Quantity	Description	Cat No	Price each £	Cost £	VAT rate %	VAT amount £
60	'Faulkner Major' frame tents	734T	260.00	15600.00		
	Less trade discount 15%			2340.00		
				13260.00	15	1989.00
	Plus VAT			1989.00		
				15249.00		
	Delivered 6/7/19--- by our van to your order at 149 High Street, Woking					

Fig 27   A sales invoice

5 The quantities, terms and extensions are checked by another member of staff in the Invoice
Section.

6 The invoice set is typed using carbon paper or
NCR (no carbon required) paper to reproduce
the copies.

The sales invoice prepared for Brentfords' order
is given in Fig 27.

Exercises

1 Make out the invoices which P Faulkner & Sons would prepare for the three orders confirmed in Section 4.2, Exercise **1** (p 45). Assume that they were invoiced exactly on the delivery times stated and allocate appropriate reference numbers.

2 Prepare invoices dated 12 July 19— for the following customers (refer to the price list on p 39, the customer records on p 43 and the order book on p 44 for relevant data):

Customer	Order No	Quantity	Cat No	Invoice No
Arnold & Baker	S63720	10	79C	1629
Attwood Camping Distributors plc	S63721	6	754T	
		6	774T	1630
Bell & Sons	S63722	50	523T	
		40	553T	1631
Brown & Co Ltd	S63723	10	27R	1632
Hugh Charles	S63724	8	79C	1633
David Coleman (Sports Equipment) Ltd	S63725	10	523T	
		10	553T	1634

3 *a* Draw up an invoice for the following transaction:

On 27 June 19— Wilton, Watkins and Irvine Ltd, 93 Bowling Street, Sheffield, sold to Philip Hayes, 391 Petre Road, Ipswich, the following goods:

12 reams Brooklyn Bond paper
            @ £2.50 a ream
24 reams Flimsy paper   @ £1.70 a ream
18 reams Brooklyn Duplicating
   paper   @ £1.90 a ream
12 typewriter ribbons   @ £1.25 each
12 typewriter erasers   @ 25p each

Terms: 5% 7 days, 2½% 30 days.

b What do the following terms and abbreviations mean: 5% 7 days, 2½% 30 days?

c Why does the seller of goods send out invoices?

d Give *two* ways in which an invoice differs from a statement. (*RSA OPI*)

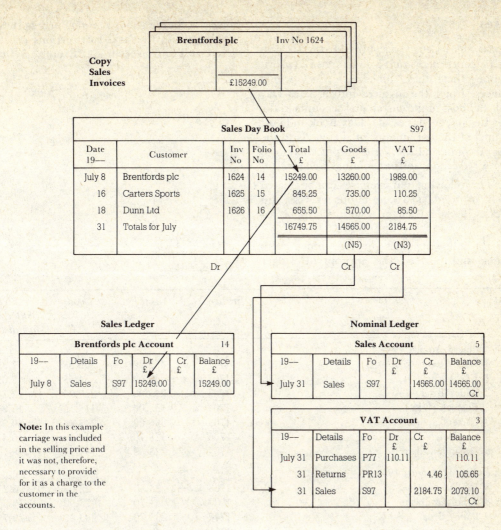

Copy Sales Invoices

Brentfords plc	Inv No 1624
	£15249.00

Sales Day Book S97

Date 19—	Customer	Inv No	Folio No	Total £	Goods £	VAT £
July 8	Brentfords plc	1624	14	15249.00	13260.00	1989.00
16	Carters Sports	1625	15	845.25	735.00	110.25
18	Dunn Ltd	1626	16	655.50	570.00	85.50
31	Totals for July			16749.75	14565.00	2184.75
					(N5)	(N3)
				Dr	Cr	Cr

Sales Ledger

Brentfords plc Account 14

19—	Details	Fo	Dr £	Cr £	Balance £
July 8	Sales	S97	15249.00		15249.00

Note: In this example carriage was included in the selling price and it was not, therefore, necessary to provide for it as a charge to the customer in the accounts.

Nominal Ledger

Sales Account 5

19—	Details	Fo	Dr £	Cr £	Balance £
July 31	Sales	S97		14565.00	14565.00 Cr

VAT Account 3

19—	Details	Fo	Dr £	Cr £	Balance £
July 31	Purchases	P77	110.11		110.11
31	Returns	PR13		4.46	105.65
31	Sales	S97		2184.75	2079.10 Cr

Fig 28 Procedure for dealing with sales invoices

5.2 Sales Day Book and Ledger

The Sales Ledger contains the personal accounts of all the firm's customers (debtors). Only goods sold on credit are entered in the Sales Day Book; cash sales are entered in the Bank Account, and the sale on credit of assets, such as surplus furniture or equipment, would be entered in a separate journal. The procedure involved in entering the invoice to Brentfords' Account is shown in Fig 28.

The steps are:

1 Enter the copy sales invoice in the Sales Day Book as in the example given.
2 Transfer the total value of the invoice to the debit column of Brentfords' Account in the Sales Ledger as they *received* the goods and are, therefore, *debtors*, ie customers who owe the firm for goods supplied.
3 At the end of the month the three columns of the Sales Day Book are totalled. The total for the net value of the goods is credited to the Sales Account and the total of the VAT output tax is credited to the VAT Account in the Nominal Ledger. The VAT account will have both debit and credit entries and may have a debit balance or, as would be expected in the case of P Faulkner & Sons, a credit balance because the value of their sales would normally exceed the value of their purchases and expenses.

Exercises

1 Prepare Sales Ledger accounts for the six customers named in Section 5.1, Exercise **2** (p 48). Assume that they all had nil opening balances. Enter the invoices into a Sales Day Book and post to the customers' accounts in the Sales Ledger, total the Sales Day Book and post the total of the net amount of the goods to the Sales Account and the VAT output charges to the VAT Account in the Nominal Ledger.

Note: The following four exercises can be treated separately or used as a continuous exercise (in which case 10 Sales Ledger accounts will be required).

Enter the following sales invoices into a Sales Day Book and post to the appropriate ledger accounts:

These accounts should be retained as they will be used again in the next two sections (Section 5.3, Exercise **1** and Section 5.4, Exercise **5**).

Date 19—	Customer	Invoice No	Total	Goods	VAT (after 2½% cash discount)
			£	£	£
2 Week ending 5 August 19—					
Aug 1	N K Aldous & Sons	1701	453.20	395.38	57.82
1	J G Andrews	1702	39.60	34.55	5.05
2	Bailey Bros	1703	253.00	220.73	32.27
2	Bostock (DIY)	1704	132.00	115.16	16.84
3	Carters Sports	1705	396.00	345.48	50.52
4	Chudleigh & Sons	1706	128.70	112.29	16.41
5	Dreamland Ltd	1707	225.50	196.74	28.76
3 Week ending 12 August 19—					
Aug 8	J G Andrews	1708	25.30	22.08	3.22
8	Arnold & Baker	1709	84.70	73.90	10.80
9	Bailey Bros	1710	233.20	203.45	29.75
9	Carters Sports	1711	49.50	43.19	6.31
9	Chudleigh & Sons	1712	795.30	693.84	101.46
12	David Coleman (Sports Equipment) Ltd	1713	479.60	418.42	61.18
4 Week ending 19 August 19—					
Aug 15	N K Aldous & Sons	1714	16.50	14.40	2.10
16	Bailey Bros	1715	586.52	511.70	74.82
16	Bostock (DIY)	1716	876.92	765.05	111.87
16	Carters Sports	1717	123.20	107.49	15.71
16	David Coleman (Sports Equipment) Ltd	1718	51.70	45.11	6.59
17	Dreamland Ltd	1719	630.96	550.47	80.49
18	Dunn (Sports Outfitters) Ltd	1720	475.20	414.58	60.62
5 Week ending 26 August 19—					
Aug 22	Arnold & Baker	1721	1 657.70	1 446.22	211.48
22	Bailey Bros	1722	254.10	221.69	32.41
22	Bostock (DIY)	1723	55.00	47.99	7.01
24	Carters Sports	1724	838.20	731.27	106.93
25	Chudleigh & Sons	1725	1 228.70	1 071.95	156.75
25	Dreamland Ltd	1726	4 407.70	3 845.37	562.33
25	Dunn (Sports Outfitters) Ltd	1727	762.30	665.05	97.25

6 *a* Clearly distinguish between VAT inputs and VAT outputs.

b A Wise made the following purchases and sales on credit during the three months ended 31 December 198—:

Purchases
198— Oct £6 000 + VAT   *900*
        Nov £8 000 + VAT   *1200*
        Dec £9 000 + VAT   *1350*
                      3450

Sales
Oct £9 000 + VAT   *1350*
Nov £10 000 + VAT   *1500*
Dec £15 000 + VAT   *2250*
VAT is to be taken at the rate of 10% *5700*

Prepare the VAT Account of A Wise for the three months ended 31 December 198—. Any outstanding amount payable to the Customs and Excise should be remitted by cheque on 31 December 198—.   (*RSA BKI*)

£1650 to pay.

5.3 Sales returns

The Purchases Department occasionally has to deal with returns in respect of goods sent back to suppliers or for claims on them for complaints such as short delivery, ie below the invoiced quantity, inferior quality, damaged goods and invoice errors (see p 19). Whatever the reason for the 'return', the supplier has to provide a credit note and the transaction is called a **purchases return**. P Faulkner & Sons were themselves also required to supply a credit note when a claim for an allowance was agreed with a customer. Because the firm took pride in its workmanship and goods were inspected before despatch, together with the system of checking invoices before sending them out, the need to issue credit notes was rare.

One such occasion did, however, arise in connection with the delivery of the 60 'Faulkner Major' frame tents to Brentfords plc on 8 July 19—. When Brentfords opened the packages it was discovered that some of the metal poles were bent and the stitching had split in a few places. Faulkners were not sure whether it was the fault of their driver who had helped to load them on the delivery van or whether the damage was due to careless handling by Brentfords. In any event, as Brentfords were good regular customers and Faulkners were anxious to retain their goodwill, it was decided to agree to the return of the two damaged tents and to issue Brentfords with a credit note (Fig 29, p 52). Note that this document would be printed in red to draw attention to the credit effect.

Although sales returns were rare, Mr D Faulkner insisted that they were to be recorded separately and each item, even if it was only an arithmetical error, had to be brought to his attention as he was very keen to preserve the good reputation of the firm. The procedure for recording sales returns is illustrated in Fig 30 on p 53.

The credit note is typed and checked with the original sales invoice, particular attention being paid to any trade discount which is deducted, as shown on p 47.

Four copies of the credit note are prepared, for the following reasons:

1   **Customer** receives the top copy
2   **Accounts** (Sales Ledger Section) for entry into the customer's account
3   **Sales** for filing and linking with the order and invoice
4   **Sales** copy for Sales Manager's personal attention

CREDIT NOTE

No 12

From: P FAULKNER & SONS, Chestnut Avenue, Southampton SO2 4AG

Tel: 0703 7654321   Telex: FA 7812
VAT Registration No 3043739 11   Date: 28 July 19—
                                           Ref: Invoice No 1624
                                               dated   8/7/19—

To: Brentfords plc   Original Supply: Sale
        Weston House,
        Piccadilly,
        London W1V 9PA

Quantity	Details	Price each £	Amount £	VAT rate %	VAT amount £
2	'Faulkner Major' frame tents returned damaged	260.00 each	520.00		
	Less trade discount 15%		78.00		
			442.00	15	66.30
	Plus VAT		66.30		
			508.30		
	Received via British Rail 27 July 19—				

Fig 29   A credit note

   The Sales Ledger clerk enters the copy of the
credit note in the Sales Returns Book, as in the
example given on p 53. Because the goods are 'given
back' by the customer his personal account is
credited in the Sales Ledger, which has the effect
of cancelling part of the sale and reducing the
amount owing by him. At the end of the month the
Sales Returns Book is totalled and cross-balanced,
the total value of the goods is *debited* to a Sales
Returns Account (the firm's 'receiving' account)
and the total value of VAT is *debited* to a VAT
Account in the Nominal Ledger.

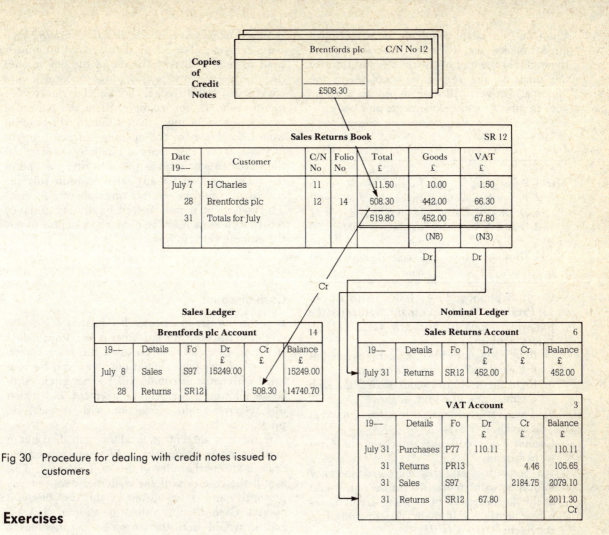

Fig 30 Procedure for dealing with credit notes issued to customers

Exercises

1 This exercise should be incorporated with Exercises **2–5** in Section 5.2 (p 50) using the same customers' accounts.

   a Prepare credit notes for the customers listed below with the information supplied.

   b Enter the credit notes in a Sales Returns Book and post to the appropriate ledger accounts.

Date 19—	Customer	Credit note No	Credit note total £	Net value of goods £	VAT £	Original No	Invoice date	Reason for credit
Sept 7	Arnold & Baker	13	8.05	7.00	1.05	1709	8.9.19—	1 rucksack returned – buckles missing
14	Chudleigh & Sons	14	57.50	50.00	7.50	1712	9.8.19—	1 tent returned damaged
20	N K Aldous & Sons	15	1.15	1.00	0.15	1714	15.8.19—	Error in calculation of invoice

2 Enter the following documents in the appropriate day books, post to the ledger accounts, total the books at the end of the month and transfer the totals to the respective accounts in the Nominal Ledger. Allocate appropriate reference numbers for the documents and books.

Date	Customer	Document	Goods	VAT
			£	£
Mar 1	Bailey Bros	Invoice	105.00	15.75
2	Brown & Co Ltd	Invoice	29.50	4.42
4	Dreamland Ltd	Invoice	64.80	9.72
8	Brown & Co Ltd	Credit note	8.00	1.20
11	Dreamland Ltd	Credit note	30.00	4.50

3 a On 10 September 19—, John Smith Ltd of 13 Packham Road, Southam, returned the following goods to Burke & Co, 14 High Street, Dublin:
  i Four 3 kW immersion heaters invoiced at £12 each less 20% trade discount
  ii Eight thermostats – retail price £9.50 each – same trade discount as above
  iii Three returnable packing cases charged at £2 each.
  Complete a credit note to cover these returned items.
b It is sometimes said that increased efficiency in dealing with an original transaction would avoid the necessity of sending credit notes subsequently. Comment briefly on this statement. (RSA OPII)

5.4 Payment for sales, including credit control and bad debts

It is a curious concept of accounting that the figure of sales is used to calculate the profit, even if the money for those sales has not been received. Although a business may be making profits, unless these are translated into money the firm cannot pay its way for long and would soon be made bankrupt. This part of a firm's operations is, therefore, most important; no matter how many sales there are and whatever the stated profit, if the sales are not paid for there would soon be no business.

The sale to Brentfords plc was due for payment on 8 August 19—, but as a credit note had been issued by P Faulkner & Sons, Brentfords were only required to pay £14 740.70, ie Sales: £15 249.00 – Sales returns: £508.30. A statement of account is used to remind Brentfords plc of the net amount due for payment (Fig 31). This document is a copy of the Sales Ledger Account for the current month only. If, for example, there was a sum of money owing for more than a month, the amount would be shown in the opening balance brought forward. It was customary at Faulkners to send out the statements as soon as possible after the end of the month so that for any sales made in July the statement would be sent out on or about 3 August. The statement is not entered in any accountancy record as it is merely a reminder to a debtor to pay the amount outstanding.

Cash discount

It is the normal practice of P Faulkner & Sons to give cash discount if a customer pays within 7 days of the invoice, as referred to in the price list on p 39. *Cash* discount should not, however, be confused with *trade* discount, which is not intended to be an allowance for prompt payment and which was referred to in connection with invoices on pp 12 and 46.

If there is agreement to allow cash discount it must be made before the invoice is prepared because it affects the value of the VAT charged. This is still the case even if the customer does not pay promptly and take advantage of the discount offered. Cash discount cannot be allowed on VAT and it would not, therefore, be permissible to deduct it from the net amount of a statement which had a VAT charge included in it.

Fig 32 on p 56 is an example of an invoice on which cash discount is allowed. The calculation of the invoice price is as follows:

	£
10 'Faulkner Ranger' tents @ £130.00 each	= 1 300.00

Cash discount of 5% on the value of the goods

$$\frac{5}{100} \times \frac{1\,300}{1} = \frac{65}{1} \qquad = \quad 65.00$$

Value of goods for VAT purposes = £1 300 – £65	= 1 235.00
VAT at 15% on £1 235	= 185.25
Net value of invoice = £1 300 + £185.25	= 1 485.25
Net amount payable if cash discount is taken = £1 485.25 – £65.00	= 1 420.25

STATEMENT

From: P FAULKNER & SONS, Chestnut Avenue, Southampton SO2 4AG

Telephone: 0703 7654321   Telex: FA7812

To: Brentfords plc
     Weston House
     Piccadilly
     London W1V 9PA   Date: 31 July 19—

Terms: Net cash within one month after delivery

Date	Details	Ref No	Dr £	Cr £	Balance £
19— July 8	Sales	1624	15249.00		15249.00
28	Returns	12		508.30	14740.70

The last amount in the balance column is the amount owing
Please return this statement with your remittance.

Fig 31   A statement of account

```
                            INVOICE

                                                No  1813

              P FAULKNER & SONS, Chestnut Avenue, Southampton SO2 4AG


   Tel:  0703 7654321                    Telex: FA7812

   VAT Registration No  3043739 11       Date: 7 September 19---

   To:  ┌─────────────────────────┐      Supply:  Sale
        │   Donald Dentford Ltd    │
        │   1 High Road            │
        │   Wormley               │
        │   Broxbourne, Herts     │
        │   BE3 8AS               │
        └─────────────────────────┘

   Terms:  5% cash discount for payment within 7 days
           Delivery Broxbourne

   Completion of Order No  S93421  dated  14 August 19---
```

Quantity	Description	Cat No	Price each £	Cost £	VAT rate %	VAT amount £
10	'Faulkner Ranger' tents	553T	130.00	1300.00	15	185.25
	Plus VAT			185.25		
				1485.25		

```
   Net cash within 7 days: £1420.25
```

Fig 32   An invoice

It will be seen, therefore, that not only does Donald Dentford Ltd save £65 on the goods by paying early but also another £9.75 on the VAT charged. Without cash discount the invoice would be £1 300 + VAT @ 15% (£195) = £1 495.00. Where trade discount is deducted the remaining value is used in calculating any cash discount.

Discount allowed to customers is credited in the customer's account to reduce the amount due and debited in a discount allowed account because the amount allowed to the customer is an expense to the firm. Cash discount allowed by suppliers would be called discount received and the entries in the accounts would be reversed. Further information on cash discounts is given in Section 6.1 (p 73).

Credit control

A sale is not complete until the transaction is finally paid for. The delivery of the goods and despatch of the invoice, still less the receipt of an order, does not constitute a completed sale. It is vital that everything is done to ensure that payment is received and bad debts avoided; in a bad debt not only is the profit lost but the VAT still has to be paid by the seller to Customs and Excise. Furthermore, as the cost of the goods may be 10 times the profit, eg Cost £100 + Profit £10 = Selling Price £110, 10 sales of the same value would be needed simply to recover the cost from one bad debt. Credit control is, therefore, essential and this entails:

1   Obtaining trade and bank references to discover if customers are creditworthy – further details of credit approval were given on p 42
2   Drawing up a schedule of customers with the amounts owing for each transaction at the end of the month

3   Marking the items off when paid
4   Transferring the amounts in 'arrears' columns when necessary, ie one month overdue, etc
5   Sending additional reminders to the customers, eg a first reminder to a customer who normally pays promptly could have stamped on the statement:

A Reminder

that this account has probably been overlooked. We would appreciate your early remittance. Thank you.

---

6   When an account is three months overdue sending a memorandum to Mr D Faulkner, advising him of the situation.

An extract from the schedule of customers at 30 June is given in Fig 33. Several items are deleted to indicate that cheques have been received at 14 July 19—, but I N Credit & Co have not paid the £34 which was owing by them as long ago as 1 January. Several statements and reminders have been sent to them. Mr D Faulkner has telephoned and written to them and in spite of promises by the firm to pay, no payment had been made. At this stage Mr D Faulkner might decide to pass the case over to Mr S Faulkner, who would consult the firm's solicitors with a view to legal proceedings being taken to recover the debt due.

Schedule of Customers A to D				30 June 19--
Customer	3 months overdue	2 months overdue	1 month overdue	Current
	£	£	£	£
N K Aldous & Sons			~~67.00~~	~~73.00~~ 47.00
J G Andrews			~~54.00~~	120.00
Bailey Bros			~~63.00~~	~~225.00~~ 76.00
I N Credit & Co	34.00			

Fig 33   Schedule of customers

Bad debts

A debt due from a customer may be considered as being irrecoverable for several reasons, eg the customer may be bankrupt (unable to pay his debts) or may have 'gone away' and cannot be traced, or the amount involved is small and has been owing for some time, say six months, and the cost of trying to recover the money due is as much as, or more, than the debt itself. Whatever the reason the business may recognise that to keep a worthless debt due from a customer in the books is pointless and misleading, and the debt should be written off as follows:

Sales Ledger

I N Credit & Co Account					130
19--	Details	Fo	Dr £	Cr £	Balance £
Jan 1	Sales	S	34.00		34.00
Aug 7	Payment	CPJ		10.00	24.00
31	Bad debts			24.00	—

Nominal ledger

Bad Debts Account					42
19--	Details	Fo	Dr £	Cr £	Balance £
Aug 31	I N Credit & Co		24.00		24.00

In this case it was decided to write-off I N Credit & Co's debt of £24.00 by crediting I N Credit & Co to indicate that they had 'given' a bad debt, whilst the bad debts account was debited to show that P Faulkner & Sons had 'received' a bad debt.

Cash receipts

The staff of the Sales Ledger Section do not actually see the cheques coming into the firm. For purposes of security and for spreading the work, they are handled by the cashier – see Section 6.

The Sales Ledger Section must, however, receive notification of the receipts so that they can enter them in the customers' ledger accounts. The procedure adopted by P Faulkner & Sons for recording receipts is as follows:

1 All cheques received are entered in a Cash Receipts Journal by a clerk in the Cashier's Section and the cheques are paid into the bank. The payments into the Bank Account are dealt with later.
2 A copy of the Cash Receipts Journal, together with any returned statements or other advices of payment, is sent to the Sales Ledger Section for each day's transactions.
3 The customers' accounts in the Sales Ledger are credited with the receipts.
4 The receipts are marked off on the schedule of customers.

An example of the Cash Receipts Journal for 8 August, together with the posting procedure is shown in Fig 34.

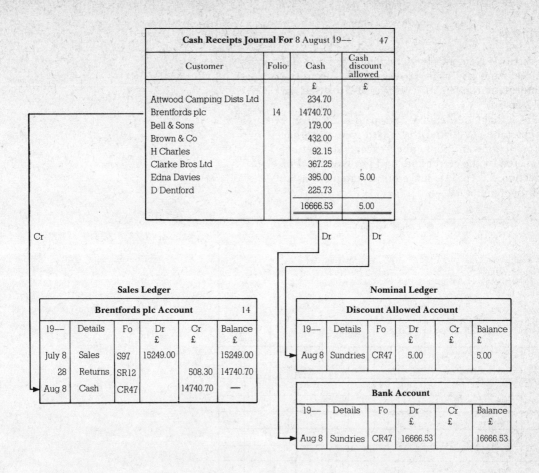

Fig 34   Cash Receipts Journal and posting procedure

Exercises

1 Prepare statements for Chudleigh & Sons and Dreamland Ltd as at 31 August 19— from the information given in Exercises **2–5** of Section 5.2 (p 50).

2 Given that Chudleigh & Sons paid £128.70 on 4 September 19— and that there were no other transactions in September except the return covered by the credit note no 14 in Exercise **1** of Section 5.3 (p 53), make out a statement as at 30 September 19—.

Ledger Account

Everyman Bargains Ltd   Account No:
123 High Street,
Whitley Bay, Northumberland   Credit £

Terms – 5% monthly

Date	Details	Debit £	Debit p	Credit £	Credit p	Balance £	Balance p	Old Balance £	Old Balance p
19—									
April 30	A/c rendered					25	00		
May 1	Goods	31	60					25	00
8	Goods	27	25						
15	Goods	5	00						
17	Cheque			23	75				
17	Discount			1	25				
23	Returns			4	10				
30	Goods	12	50						

3 *a i* Is the above ledger account that of a customer or a supplier?
   ii What is a remittance advice?
   iii What is a statement of account?
   iv What is usually done before a firm will grant a prospective customer a credit account?

   b Copy the ledger account and complete any unfinished details.

4 *a* Prepare invoices from the following details using the descriptions and prices quoted in the price list on p 39.

Date	Customer	Quantity	Cat No	Cash discount %
10 Sept	Baldwin Stores Ltd	10	15SB	5
17	Brown & Co Ltd	10	734T	2½
24	Edna Davies	6	774T	
		12	583T	2½
30	Dunn (Sports Outfitters) Ltd	40	27R	
		20	31R	2½

b Enter the invoices in a Sales Day Book, open ledger accounts and post to the appropriate ledger accounts, total the Sales Day Book at the end of the month and transfer the totals to the appropriate accounts in the Nominal Ledger.

5 This exercise can be used with the 10 Sales Ledger Accounts already opened in connection with Exercises **2–5** of Section 5.2 (p 50) and Exercise **1** of Section 5.3 (p 53) or it may be worked separately.

Enter the following cheques which were received by P Faulkner & Sons into a Cash Receipts Journal, total the journal after each day's cheques have been entered and post to the customers' accounts in the Sales Ledger.

Date	Customer	Amount
		£
Sept 3	N K Aldous & Sons	453.20
	Bailey Brothers	253.00
	Bostock (DIY)	132.00
	Chudleigh & Sons	128.70
	Dreamland Ltd	225.50
Sept 10	J G Andrews	64.90
	Carters Sports	445.50
	David Coleman (Sports Equipment) Ltd	479.60
Sept 17	Arnold & Baker	77.00
	Bailey Bros	819.72
	Chudleigh & Sons	740.30
	Dreamland Ltd	630.96
	Dunn (Sports Outfitters) Ltd	475.20
Sept 24	N K Aldous & Sons	15.40
	Bostock (DIY)	831.92
	Carters Sports	961.40
	Dreamland Ltd	4 407.70
	Dunn (Sports Outfitters) Ltd	762.30

6 The following is an extract from the trade catalogue of K E Stevens who are manufacturers of camping equipment.

Ref	Sleeping bags		Trade price	Recommended retail price
			£	£
A142	Super	44 oz	8.00	12.00
A143	Standard	38 oz	7.50	10.00

All prices are subject to VAT @ 10%.

On 7 April 198— P Burrows of 80 Budge Lane, Northtown, ordered 20 Super sleeping bags and 16 Standard bags by order no 726. These were despatched on 8 April 198— under invoice No 14631.

a Prepare the invoice that K E Stevens will send to P Burrows.

b Assuming that he does not give discounts to customers, calculate the retailer's gross profit on each type of sleeping bag, as a percentage of

i cost price

ii selling price

c Prepare the document that K E Stevens will send to P Burrows on the 21 April 198— when Burrows returns two Super sleeping bags as faulty and is allowed full credit for them.

d Calculate the total gross profit that Burrows will make if he sells all the sleeping bags less the two returned at the recommended price. (*RSA BKI*)

7 Enter the following transactions in the Sales Day Book. At the end of the month total the Day Book and indicate the amounts to be posted to the general ledger. All transactions are subject to VAT at 10%.

April 1	Sold office furniture to Ajax Services, list price £240 allowing them 20% trade discount. Invoice no 8723
April 8	Sold 4 filing cabinets to Markups at list price of £50 each. Invoice no 8726
April 18	Sold 6 typewriters to Jones Machines, list price £90 each. Trade discount of 15% was allowed. Invoice no 8728
April 28	Sold office furniture to Wye Products, list price £300. Trade discount of 20% was allowed. Invoice no 8734

Note: Ledger accounts are not required.

(*RSA BKI*)

8 J Pomeroy Ltd are in business as tobacco and sweet wholesalers. Open accounts in their Sales Ledger for the following customers:

		£
Abercrombie & Co	debit	175.00
Dewbar Stores	debit	403.00
L Frankfurt Ltd	debit	75.00
P Stone & Sons	credit	5.00
Trelawney Travel Supplies	—	
Watkins Supermarket Ltd	debit	503.00

The transactions listed on p 62 took place; record them in the appropriate accounting books and ledgers.

Date	Customer	Document	Serial No	Total value	Goods	VAT
				£	£	£
Dec 3	Abercrombie & Co	Invoice	1729	198.00	172.18	25.82
3	Dewbar Stores	Invoice	1730	616.00	535.66	80.34
3	Trelawney Travel Supplies	Invoice	1731	450.00	391.31	58.69
3	Watkins Supermarket Ltd	Invoice	1732	254.00	220.87	33.13
9	Abercrombie & Co	Cheque		175.00		
9	L Frankfurt Ltd	Cheque		75.00		
9	Watkins Supermarket	Cheque		307.00		
10	Dewbar Stores	Credit note	76	33.00	28.70	4.30
10	P Stone & Sons	Invoice	1733	31.90	27.74	4.16
10	Trelawney Travel Supplies	Invoice	1734	495.00	430.44	64.56
10	Watkins Supermarket	Invoice	1735	330.00	286.96	43.04
16	Dewbar Stores	Cheque		370.00		
16	Trelawney Travel Supplies	Cheque		450.00		
24	Abercrombie & Co	Invoice	1736	227.70	198.00	29.70
24	L Frankfurt Ltd	Invoice	1737	74.80	65.05	9.75
24	P Stone & Sons	Invoice	1738	44.00	38.26	5.74
24	Watkins Supermarket	Invoice	1739	275.00	239.13	35.87

9 a Copy out the credit control schedule of debtors as at 31 July 19— illustrated below then deal with the cheques received 7 August 19—, by deleting the appropriate amounts on your schedule.

Cheques received on 7 August 19—

	£
N K Aldous & Sons	47.00
J G Andrews	120.00
Bailey Bros	76.00 (Current)
I N Credit	10.00
Dreamland Ltd	196.00

b What action should be taken regarding Bailey Bros' Account?

c Rewrite the schedule for 31 August by moving the remaining figures back one month (except for the three months overdue) and adding into the current column:

	£
N K Aldous & Sons	120.00
J G Andrews	150.00
Dreamland Ltd	130.00

Check your figures by adding the schedule vertically and horizontally and double check the total by adding the new current items to the total for 31 July minus the cheques received.

Schedule of debtors A to D	as at 31 July 19—				
Customer	3 months overdue	2 months overdue	1 month overdue	Current	Totals
	£	£	£	£	£
N K Aldous & Sons			47.00	102.00	149.00
J G Andrews			120.00	76.70	196.70
Bailey Bros			76.00	76.00	152.00
I N Credit	34.00				34.00
Donald Dentford		127.60		79.00	206.60
Dreamland Ltd	120.00	76.00	54.00		250.00
	154.00	203.60	297.00	333.70	988.30

5.5 Simultaneous records and slip system

The simultaneous sales record procedure is similar to the purchases routine except that invoices are *debited* to the customers' accounts which will normally have debit opening balances.

The simultaneous record procedure for sales is as follows:

1 The copy invoices are sorted into the order required, ie alphabetically or numerically with an index.
2 A print calculator is used to add up:
   a the net value of the goods
   b the value of the VAT charged
   c the net value of the invoices which equals the combined totals of a and b. This is called pre-listing
3 A proof sheet is placed on the copywriter board (this takes the place of the Sales Day Book).
4 A sheet of carbon paper is placed over the proof sheet or NCR paper is used.
5 The customer's ledger account is selected for the first invoice and lined up with the proof sheet and placed on top of the carbon paper.
6 The customer's statement, normally containing NCR paper, is placed on top of the ledger account, providing for the entry of three records in one operation.
7 The old balance, as provided on the ledger sheet, is entered and the customer's name written on the proof sheet only. The amount of the invoice is debited and the new balance updated with the addition of the new item (the VAT and goods are usually recorded separately).
8 The customer's account sheet and statement are removed from the board, and the next customer's account and statement selected for updating.
9 When all the invoices have been posted, the columns on the proof sheet are totalled, using a print calculator, and it will be seen that:

$$\begin{matrix} \text{total of} \\ \text{old balances} \end{matrix} + \begin{matrix} \text{total of} \\ \text{debit entries} \\ \text{(both goods} \\ \text{and VAT)} \end{matrix} = \begin{matrix} \text{total of} \\ \text{new balances} \end{matrix}$$

Also

$$\begin{matrix} \text{total of} \\ \text{goods and VAT} \end{matrix} = \begin{matrix} \text{total of} \\ \text{pre-list} \end{matrix}$$

10 The totals of the pre-list, as confirmed by the totals on the proof sheet, are posted to the Nominal Ledger as follows:
   a the net value of the goods → credit → Sales Account
   b VAT → credit → VAT Account
   c the net value of the invoices → debit → Sales Ledger Control Account (to be explained in Section 5.6)
11 When customers pay their accounts, the information supplied on the Cash Receipts Journal is entered in the ledger accounts as follows:
   a the individual cheques → credit → Customer's Account
   b the total amount of cheques → debit → Bank Account
   c the total amount of cheques → credit → Sales Ledger Control Account
12 The procedure for dealing with credit notes issued to customers is as follows:
   a The credit notes are pre-listed, by using a print calculator providing totals for:
      i the net value of the goods
      ii the VAT charges and
      iii the net value of the credit notes which equal the combined totals of i and ii
   b The credit notes are credited to the customers' ledger accounts and statements.
   c The totals of the pre-list are posted to the nominal ledger as follows:
      i the net value of the goods → debit → Sales Returns Account
      ii VAT → debit → VAT Account
      iii the net value of the credit notes → credit → Sales Ledger Control Account

Fig 35 illustrates the three-in-one system for sales and sales returns.

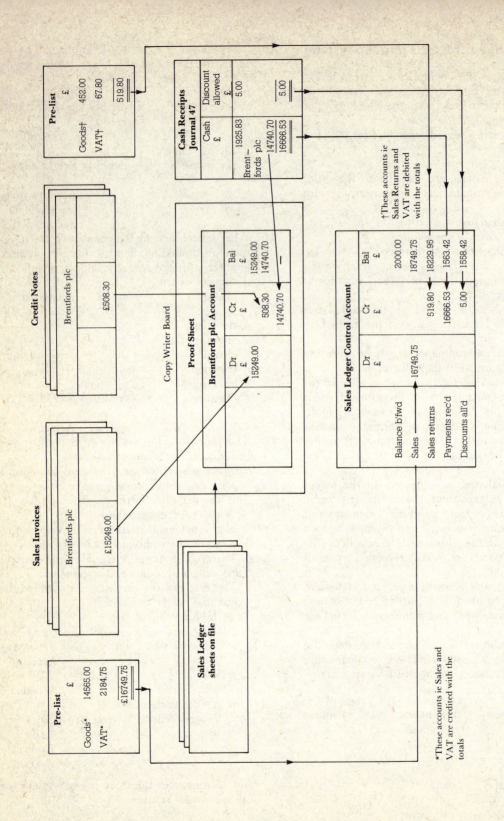

Fig 35 The three-in-one system for sales and sales returns

The slip system

It is an accepted principle in accounting practice that no entry should be made in the ledger unless it has first been entered in a book of original entry, eg the Purchases Day Book or the Sales Day Book. Some small businesses can, however, save time and money by not using day books and using instead the 'slip system' provided that:

1   the amounts owing to suppliers are paid on a regular basis such as the end of the month. In this case invoices would be filed under the due date for payment, allowance being made to take advantage of any cash discount which may be on offer

2   there is a strict system of security control for invoices and credit notes before and after payment

The procedure is illustrated in Fig 36 where it can be seen that a batch of purchases invoices (batch no 732) is pre-listed, totalling £1 725, comprising goods £1 500 and VAT £225. The total is credited to the Purchases Ledger Control Account whilst the goods are debited to the Purchases Account and the VAT input is debited to the VAT Account.

Any credit notes from suppliers can be stapled to the relevant purchases invoices and deducted from the invoice amounts. When the due date for payment arrives the cheques are made out and entered in a cash payments sheet and totalled, thus providing the information to debit the Purchases Ledger Control Account (and mark the individual invoices 'paid') and credit the Bank Account.

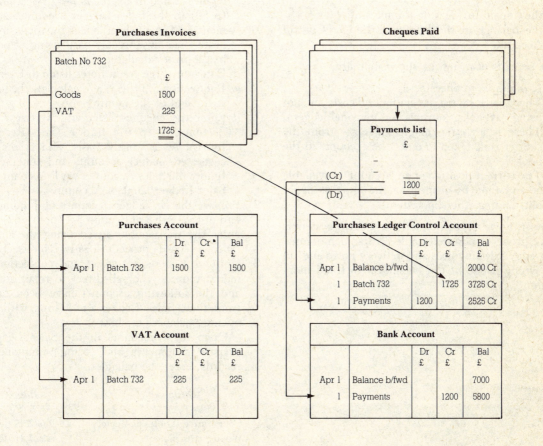

Fig 36   The slip system for purchases

A similar system would apply to the sales except that the payment dates would vary according to the different practices of the customers. Under this system the outstanding (unpaid) invoices and credit notes themselves constitute the accounts and there is no need to accumulate other items. Every week or month a check can be made as follows:

		£
a	Total the net amount of the invoices at the beginning	2 000
b	Add the total of the pre-listed invoices	1 725
		3 725
c	Deduct any credit notes received and cash paid from the Cash Book (or Cash Payments List)	1 200
		2 525

The sum remaining (£2 525 in this case) should equal:

1   the unpaid invoices on the file and
2   the balance in the Purchases Ledger Control Account

The benefits of using the slip system are:

1   It is simple to operate.
2   There is a saving in stationery costs by not using daybooks, journals and personal ledgers.
3   There is a saving in clerical costs from the shorter time taken to enter the accounts in the books.
4   The current position of an 'account' is available at any time by inspecting the slips of paper outstanding (the slip system).

It must, however, be pointed out that the system is more prone to non-detectable errors such as missing copy sales invoices and delivery notes and, in the wrong hands, it can be subject to fraud more easily.

Exercises

(*Note:* In all the questions in this section the amount of the invoice is the total amount and includes the VAT charge.)

1   *a*   Prepare Sales Ledger accounts and statements as on 1 August for the following customers with the addresses supplied in the records of customers on p 43. All have *nil* opening balances.

N K Aldous & Sons	Carters Sports
	Chudleigh & Sons
J G Andrews	David Coleman (Sports
Arnold & Baker	Equipment) Ltd
Bailey Bros	Dreamland Ltd
Bostock (DIY)	Dunn (Sports Outfitters) Ltd

b   Using a copywriter board enter the sales invoices listed in Exercises **2–5** of Section 5.2 (p 50) in the Sales Ledger accounts, statements and proof sheet, check the totals on the proof sheet on a weekly basis using, if possible, a print calculator.

c   Enter the three credit notes listed in Exercise **1** of Section 5.3 (p 53) and calculate the totals at the end of the month.

d   Enter the cheques listed in Exercise **5** of Section 5.4 (p 61) into a Cash Receipts Journal on a weekly basis, and credit the customer's ledger accounts and statements. Ignore the Sales Account, VAT Account and Sales Ledger Control Account.

2   Prepare the six ledger accounts of J Pomeroy Ltd in Exercise **8** of Section 5.4 (pp 61–62) and enter the transactions listed using the simultaneous records procedure as in Exercise **1**.

3   C Bond & Sons are sweet and confectionery manufacturers who sell direct to retail outlets and the following accounts have been taken from their Sales Ledger on 1 June with the opening balances as shown.

Open these accounts in the Sales Ledger, prepare statements and, using simultaneous records, enter the balances.

Customer	Balance
	£
Cooperative Wholesale Society	1 602.17 debit
Woolworths plc	6 927.16 debit
Pricerite Ltd	402.00 debit
Corner Supplies	12.00 credit
Debenhams plc	7 302.22 debit
NAAFI	1 407.61 debit

Date 19—	Customer	Document	Serial No	Total	Goods	VAT
				£	£	£
June 4	Cooperative Wholesale Society	Invoice	472	530.27	461.11	69.16
4	Pricerite Ltd	Invoice	473	78.40	68.18	10.22
7	Corner Supplies	Invoice	474	26.13	22.73	3.40
7	NAAFI	Invoice	475	1 257.78	1 093.73	164.05
7	Debenhams plc	Invoice	476	261.36	227.27	34.09
7	Woolworths plc	Invoice	477	1 263.49	1 094.34	169.15
17	NAAFI	Credit note	79	16.38	14.25	2.13
17	Debenhams plc	Credit note	80	211.35	183.79	27.56
				Value		
24	Cooperative Wholesale Society	Cheque	100312	1 310.00		
24	Woolworths plc	Cheque	100313	5 007.23		
24	Debenhams plc	Cheque	100314	7 302.22		
24	Corner Supplies	Cheque	100315	13.00		
24	Pricerite Ltd	Cheque	100316	402.00		

The above transactions took place; pre-list the invoices, enter them into the proper books and, using copywriter boards, post them to the appropriate accounts in the ledger and statements.

4 Many businesses today dispense with the use of formal Day Books. Explain how this may be done without affecting the double entry system. (*RSA BKI*)

5 Give a full description of the 'slip' system of book-keeping and explain how the system operates.

List three main advantages resulting from the use of the 'slip' system. (*RSA BKI*)

6 If the total debtors and total creditors accounts are regarded as part of the double-entry system, describe the methods which may be used to record the individual personal accounts.
(*RSA BKI*)

5.6 Sales Ledger Control Accounts

The necessity of keeping control accounts for purchases was explained in Section 3.7. By also keeping a Sales Ledger Control Account a business is able to ascertain the total amount of its debtors even when the individual personal accounts are not up to date. The principal benefit from this facility when the creditors figure is also used from the Purchases Ledger Control Account is that a trial balance can be prepared much earlier. If the trial balance does not agree then a check is made with the schedules of debtors and creditors; provided these agree with the control accounts' totals, then

the errors must have been made in the Nominal Ledger. Another benefit is that the final accounts can be prepared earlier.

The Sales Ledger Control Account (see Fig 37) is kept in the Nominal Ledger and represents a summary of all the items which have been posted to the Sales Ledger, for example:

1 The debit balances of the debtors (opening balances)
2 *Add* sales on credit (but not cash sales)
3 *Deduct* sales returns
4 *Deduct* cheques received
5 *Deduct* bad debts
6 *Deduct* discount allowed
7 Final balance = the balances of the debtors (closing balances)

Sales Ledger Control Account				
Date	Details	Dr £	Cr £	Balance £
19—				
Oct 1	Balance			4512.65
3	Sales	2097.70		6610.35
3	Sales returns		123.20	6487.15
10	Sales	2438.70		8925.85
14	Payments received		3712.10	5213.75
14	Bad debts		101.50	5112.25
30	Discount allowed		84.70	5027.55

Fig 37 Sales ledger control account

The procedure for opening and keeping the Sales Ledger Control Account is as follows:

1 Total the debtors at the beginning of the month and enter it as a debit balance.
2 When the proof sheet (or Sales Day Book) containing the sales invoices has been checked with the pre-list, the total of the net value of the invoices is debited to the Sales Ledger Control Account and the balance updated. The totals of the sales invoices for successive weeks are debited to the Control Account.
3 The total of the credit notes, as entered in the Sales Returns Book, is credited to the Control Account. (This can be done daily, weekly or at the end of the month.)
4 The total of the cheques received, as listed in the Cash Receipts Journal, is credited to the Control Account.
5 Bad debts are credited to the Control Account.
6 Discount allowed is credited to the Control Account.
7 The final balance, resulting from the above entries, should equal the total of all the debtors' accounts in the Sales Ledger, thus providing a check on the arithmetical accuracy of the ledger postings.

The relationship of the Sales Ledger Control Account with the other accounting records is illustrated in Fig 35 on p 64.

Exercises

1 Prepare the Sales Ledger Control Account for November for C Bond & Sons using the details given in Exercise 3 of Section 5.5 (pp 66–67).
2 Prepare the Sales Ledger Control Account for December for J Pomeroy Ltd using the details given in Exercise 8 of Section 5.4 (pp 61–62).
3 Prepare a Sales Ledger Control Account for the month of January from the following details:

		£
Jan 1	Total of debit balances in Sales Ledger	9 326.00
31	Sales on credit for the month	13 234.75
31	Sales returns for the month	469.53
31	Cheques received from debtors for the month	12 521.02

4 Prepare a Sales Ledger Control Account from the following for the month of April 198—

198—		£
April 1	Sales Ledger balances	3 953
30	Sales Journal	45 742
	Returns inwards	350
	Cheques received from debtors	41 270
	Discounts allowed	450
	Bad debts written off	1 059
	Sales Ledger balances	6 566
		(RSA BKI)

5 On 31 March 198— the following balances appeared in John Richard's Sales Ledger (W section):

	£
W Wilkins	1 200 dr
T Wright	750 dr
L Williams	325 dr

During April 198— the following transactions took place:

Credit sales		£
April 3	W Wilkins	1 370
13	T Wright	600
23	W Wilkins	450
Sales returns		
April 15	L Williams	200
24	T Wright	30

Payments received and cash discounts allowed		£	£
April 10	W Wilkins	1 170	30
	T Wright	740	10

You are to:
a write up the personal accounts of the three customers in John Richard's Sales Ledger (W section)
b write up the Sales Ledger (W section) Control Account for the month of April 198—
c reconcile the control account balance with the personal account balances (RSA BKI)

6 The following figures were extracted from the books of Pevatec & Co for April 198—:

	£
Sales Ledger balances 1 April	4 842
Purchase Ledger balances 1 April	2 182
Receipts from customers	84 804
Payments to suppliers	63 294
Sales	86 402
Purchases	64 823
Returns inwards	1 420
Returns outwards	1 210
Bad debts written-off	496
Discounts allowed	1 902
Discounts received	1 048
Sales Ledger balances 30 April	2 622
Purchase Ledger balances 30 April	1 453

Prepare a Sales Ledger Control Account and a Purchases Ledger Control Account for the month of April from the above information. (*RSA BKI*)

5.7 Analysed Sales Day Book

It is important for any business to know how its profit is made up. Consequently it is necessary to analyse the sales, purchases and costs into such categories as areas, countries, products, sales personnel, etc. This helps the management to be more efficient as they will be able to see those aspects of the business which make most profit or loss.

Although Mr Simon Faulkner could ascertain the profit from the Trading and Profit and Loss Account, he would have had little idea which products were bringing in the most profit if he had not analysed the sales of the different products. In order to see at a glance the proportion of sales for each group of products the Sales Day Book is analysed by using additional columns for tents, sleeping bags, rucksacks and camp beds. The example below of a columnar Sales Day Book, based on Exercise **2** of Section 5.2 (p 50), shows the breakdown of the sales of £1 420.33 into:

	£
Tents	820.86
Sleeping bags	375.47
Rucksacks	100.00
Camp beds	124.00
	£1 420.33

The analysis takes place at the time the sales invoice is entered into the Sales Day Book, ie the total value is entered twice – once in the total column and again under the product heading(s) and VAT.

Columnar books with analysis columns may also be used for purchases to analyse the cost of materials; the Cash Book, to provide a breakdown of receipts and payments for ledger sections, eg A–D; and the Petty Cash Book, for analysing expenses, as explained in Section 6.4.

Columnar Sales Day Book									
Date 19—	Customer	Inv No	Folio	Total £	Tents £	Sleeping bags £	Rucksacks £	Camp beds £	VAT £
August 1	N K Aldous & Sons	1701		453.20	395.38				57.82
1	J G Andrews	1702		39.60		34.55			5.05
2	Bailey Bros	1703		253.00	100.00	120.73			32.27
2	Bostock (DIY)	1704		132.00	80.00	35.16			16.84
3	Carters Sports	1705		396.00	245.48		100.00		50.52
4	Chudleigh & Sons	1706		128.70		88.29		24.00	16.41
5	Dreamland Ltd	1707		225.50		96.74		100.00	28.76
				£1628.00	820.86	375.47	100.00	124.00	207.67

Debit each customer

Credit Sales Account

Credit VAT Account

Total of debits = £1628.00 = £1420.33 + £207.67

Fig 38 Columnar Sales Day Book

Exercises

1   Using the same rulings as on p 69 enter the invoices listed in Exercise **3** of Section 5.2 (p 50) into an analysed Sales Day Book and cross balance. The products on the invoices were:

Invoice No	Product
1708	Sleeping bags
1709	Tents
1710	Tents
1711	Rucksacks
1712	£400 sleeping bags and £293.84 camp beds
1713	Rucksacks

2   Enter the invoices prepared in Exercise **2** of Section 5.1 (p 48) into an analysed Sales Day Book, using appropriate analysis columns for the products invoiced.

3   You are employed by John Briggs, a wholesaler in electrical appliances. The principal sales lines are televisions, radios and refrigerators.

Trade discount is allowed on televisions and refrigerators of 20%; radios 15%; and on other electrical goods 10%.

Credit sales, at catalogue prices for 2 and 3 October 19—, were as follows:

Oct 2	J Rolfe	6 radios at £50 each
	R Forber	2 televisions at £240 each
		4 refrigerators at £172 each
		6 radios at £56 each
3	D Miller	12 refrigerators at £180 each
		6 electric fans at £45 each
	K Shaw	4 televisions at £295 each
		2 electric fires at £60 each

You are required to:
a write up a suitably analysed Sales Day Book for 2 and 3 October
b state which Nominal Ledger posting should be made from the Sales Day Book (*RSA BKI*)

4   D Withers is a wholesaler. The following credit transactions took place during the month of May 198—. Enter each transaction in the appropriate book of original entry, total for the month and post to the Purchases, Sales, Returns and VAT Accounts in the ledger.

All amounts given are before the addition of VAT, which is to be taken as 10%.

All trade purchases are allowed a trade discount of 20%, not yet taken into account in the figures given below.

Trade discount is not allowed on any sales.

198—		£
May 1	Purchased stock from T Smithers Ltd	400
3	Sold stock to W Wilkin	350
4	Sold stock to T Wilson	300
11	Returned stock bought on 1 May 198— to T Smithers Ltd	50
12	Purchased stationery for office use from Paper Co Ltd	150
14	Purchased office furniture from Office Supplies Ltd	400
20	T Wilson returned stock	20
29	Sold stock to W Wilkin	170
29	Purchased stock from T Smithers Ltd	150

(*RSA BKI*)

6 Accounts – Cashier's Section

6.1 Columnar Cash Book and posting to ledger accounts

Every organisation handles cash in one form or another and those responsible for it are conscious of the need to have accurate and up-to-date cash and bank figures. This is necessary so that the organisation knows whether it will be able to meet its current financial demands. Wages, salaries and creditors must be paid on time to avoid serious difficulties; even if profits are being made, unless there is an adequate supply of money, the organisation will soon be unable to continue in business.

Cash and bank records, a Cash Account and a Bank Account will have to be kept. The Cash Book is an extension of the ledger system and no other sources are kept to record the same information, ie no Cash Account nor Bank Account in the Nominal Ledger. The records may, however, consist of a Cash Account and a Bank Account incorporated into a two-column Cash Book for convenience.

In Fig 39 the business has £50 in cash and £2 000 in its current account at the bank on 1 July. During the first week of July these transactions took place:

July 2   Paid travelling expenses in cash £12
3   Paid by cheque £500 to settle the amount owing to A Small, a supplier
4   Paid £10 in cash for Calor gas to heat storeroom
5   Received a cheque for £120 from B Round (a customer) in settlement of his account
6   Received £21 in cash for sales
6   Paid by cheque £400 to T Coles, a supplier, to settle his account
6   The Cash and Bank Accounts were balanced and the balances carried down in the Cash Book

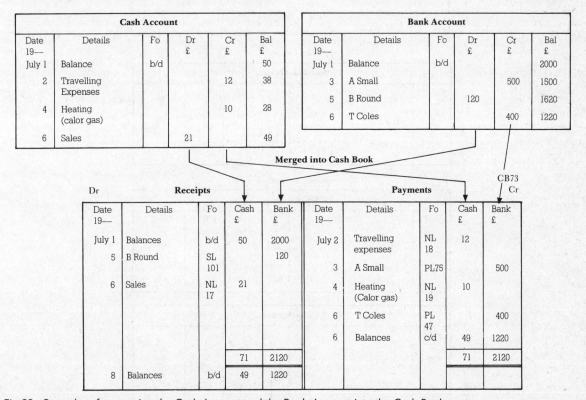

Fig 39   Procedure for merging the Cash Account and the Bank Account into the Cash Book

Note that the entries are made in date order on *two* sides, the left-hand side (Dr) for money coming in – receipts, and the right-hand side (Cr) for money paid out – payments. At the end of the week or month both accounts are 'balanced off', which involves making the totals equal for both cash and bank by means of a 'balancing entry', £49 for cash and £1 220 for the bank. The balance is the difference between the larger and smaller sides. For example, the larger amount of cash (£71) is on the Dr side. The Cr side is added up (£22) and subtracted from £71 to arrive at the balance of £49. The balancing entry is taken out of one period (week or month) and transferred to the next. To complete the double entry and provide starting figures for the next period these ledger entries are made:

Nominal Ledger

Sales Account		(17)			
Date 19––	Details	Fo	Dr £	Cr £	Bal £
July 6	Cash payment	CB 73		21	21 Cr

Travelling Expenses Account		(18)			
Date 19––	Details	Fo	Dr £	Cr £	Bal £
July 2	Payment	CB 73	12		12

Lighting and Heating Account		(19)			
Date 19––	Details	Fo	Dr £	Cr £	Bal £
July 4	Payment	CB 73	10		10

Sales Ledger

B Round Account		(101)			
Date 19––	Details	Fo	Dr £	Cr £	Bal £
July 1	Balance	b/d			120
5	Payment	CB 73		120	—

Purchases Ledger

A Small Account		(75)			
Date 19––	Details	Fo	Dr £	Cr £	Bal £
July 1	Balance	b/d			500
3	Payment	CB 73	500		—

T Coles Account		(47)			
Date 19––	Details	Fo	Dr £	Cr £	Bal £
July 1	Balance	b/d			400
6	Payment	CB 73	400		—

The folio numbers in the Cash Book cross reference to either the Nominal Ledger (for accounts other than customers and suppliers) and the Sales/Purchases Ledger for the personal accounts of customers and suppliers. In a similar manner the Nominal and Personal Ledgers indicate that the information has been transferred from the Cash Book page 73 (CB73). In this way the double entry is completed and the ledger accounts have the same basic information provided in the Cash Book.

Cash discount and the columnar Cash Book

Cash discount provides an allowance for prompt payment to customers (discount allowed) or by suppliers (discount received). The Day Book details for discount are entered in additional columns in the Cash Book. Any columns which are incorporated in a Cash Book to provide such details are known as memorandum columns.

To complete the double entry, discount allowed to customers, after being entered in a discount allowed column of the Cash Book, is debited in total to a Discount Allowed Account and the customers' accounts are credited individually. Discount received from suppliers, after being entered in a discount received column of the Cash Book is credited in total to a Discount Received Account and the suppliers' accounts are debited individually. The following illustrates the use of discount columns in a three-column Cash Book and posting the entries to ledger accounts:

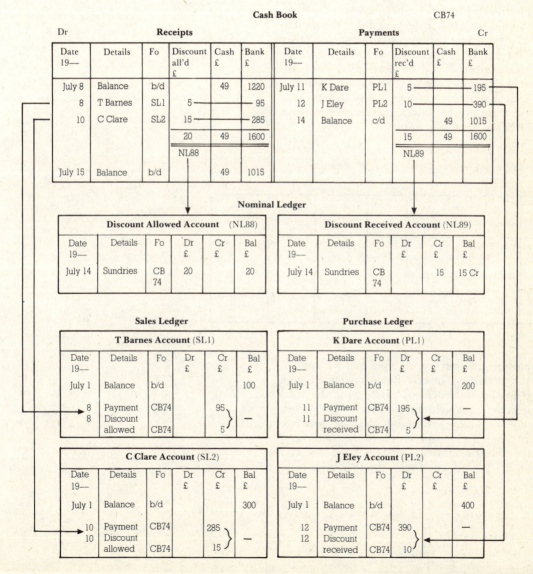

Cash Book — CB74

VAT and the Cash Book

Faulkners use the system of Cash Receipts Journals and Cash Payments Journals to simplify the task of recording cash and cheque receipts and cheque payments for their customers and suppliers. The VAT in these transactions is recorded in the Sales and Purchases Day Books. VAT is, however, charged on many other items of income and expenditure; if it has not been recorded in a day book it will have to be shown in the Cash Book. Faulkners usually pay their 'expense' invoices for such items as stationery and motor expenses on the 20th of the month and analyse the information in the details column as illustrated in the example of their analysed Bank Account/Cash Book (Fig 40). Once the Cash Receipts and Cash Payments Journal transfers have been made to the Bank Account and the other ledger accounts the double entry is completed. It only remains for the 'other items' for August to be posted as indicated to the nine accounts. It should be noted that the bank balance at 29 August was £11 938.30 and it was not until 2 September, when the bank statement was received, that the other information was known and entered in the August account.

Extract of receipts side of an analysed Bank Account

Dr

19—	Details	Fo	Discount allowed £	Bank £	Analysis of receipts £
Sept 2	Sales (cash)	NL			47.00
	B Williams	SL			105.00
	P McDonald	SL	5.00		95.00
				247.00	

The analysis column for receipts can be used to give the details of several items contained in a paying-in slip in order to match with the total shown in the bank column. The individual ledger accounts would be credited with their separate amounts, eg P McDonald with both the payment of £95 and the discount of £5. The Bank Account column has been debited with the total paid in of £247.00.

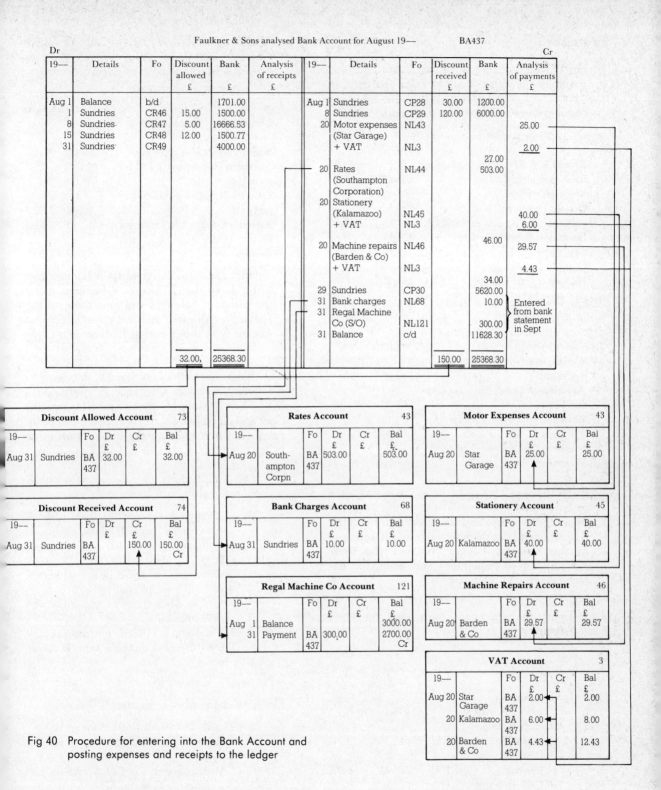

Fig 40 Procedure for entering into the Bank Account and posting expenses and receipts to the ledger

Exercises

1 On 1 September 19— the Bank Account of P Faulkner & Sons had a debit balance of £11 628.30. During September the following cheques were received and payments made:

Cheques received on 11 September

	£
Arnold & Baker	150.00
Baldwin Stores Ltd	205.05
Brentfords plc	48.10
Donald Dentford	750.00

Cheques paid on 25 September

	£
Insulation Supply Co Ltd	343.00
CIC plc	14.85
Outdoor Fabrics plc	106.50
Darling & Son Ltd	241.30

Cheques paid for expenses on 18 September		VAT included
Southern Electricity Board for electricity	60.00	Nil
Wessex Insurance Co Ltd for insurance	106.00	Nil
Star Garage Ltd for motor expenses	36.00	4.69
W H Smith & Sons Ltd for stationery	28.40	3.70
Southern Newspapers Ltd for advertising	17.00	Nil

Enter the above transactions in the appropriate cash journals and post to the Bank Account. Enter the expenses and the VAT into the Bank Account and post them to the relevant accounts in the Nominal Ledger. Balance the Bank Account on 30 September and bring the balance down on 1 October.

2 *a* Enter the following items in the Bank Account:

19—		Fo	Amount £	Discount £
Jan 1	Balance in Bank Account		1 075.00 Dr	
2	Cash Receipts Journal	CR52	149.50	3.70
3	Cash Receipts Journal	CR53	228.41	6.92
4	Cash Receipts Journal	CR54	1 052.00	23.50
5	Cash Payments Journal	CP101	341.60	15.07

b Enter the following items in the Bank Account and post them to the relevant accounts in the Nominal Ledger:

Cheques paid for expenses on 6 January	Total £	VAT included £
Southern Gas Board for gas	64.00	Nil
Southern Insurance Co Ltd for insurance	108.00	Nil
E Colley & Sons for building repairs	60.00	7.82
Red Star Garage Ltd for petrol	12.40	1.62
British Telecom for telephone charges	58.00	7.56

c Balance the Bank Account on 6 January and bring down the balance on 7 January. Total the discount columns and post them to the Discount Allowed and Discount Received Accounts in the Nominal Ledger.

3 The Bank Cash Book of James Robinson, a wholesaler, showed a balance at the bank of £684.55 on 1 May. He pays all receipts into the bank and all payments are by cheque, except for petty cash items. From the information given below, write up Robinson's Bank Cash Book:

a i The counterfoils of his paying-in book show:

May 2 Total Paid in £247.03, consisting of cash from sales £47.00, a cheque from B Williams for £105.03, and a cheque from P Mackay for £95. Mackay's cheque was accepted in full settlement of £100 owed by him

3 Paid in £103.47, consisting entirely of cash from sales

4 Total paid in £107.41, consisting of cash sales £45, and a cheque from H Roper £62.41

ii The cheque book counterfoils show:

May 2 ABC Properties Ltd £25 for rent

3 Rayon (UK) Ltd £164 for goods for resale

5 Williamson & Co Ltd £71.25 in full settlement of a debt, £75

Petty cash £24

Drawings £35

Stanfield Motors £54.17

b For each of the following transactions state the other accounts involved and the particular ledgers where these accounts may be found:

   i May 2 Cheque book counterfoil for rent £25
   ii   5 Cheque book counterfoil for Williamson & Co Ltd, £71.25 in full settlement of our debt of £75   (*RSA BKI*)

4 Memorandum columns and control accounts both have a useful role to play in book-keeping. With the aid of examples:
a briefly describe the purpose of control accounts
b explain the role of memorandum columns in a Cash Book   (*RSA BKI*)

5 The accounts which appear on 1 June 19— in the ledger of R Wilson, a stationery wholesaler, include the following:

	£
M Porcher, a customer, balance	200 debit
S Seaman, a customer, balance	75 debit
L Tidmarsh, a supplier, balance	43 credit
A Waters, a supplier, balance	75 credit
Stock of stationery in hand for own office use valued at	20

The following transactions took place during the first week of June 19—:

19—		£
June 1	Sold goods on credit to M Porcher	270
	Bought goods on credit from L Tidmarsh	75
2	Returned goods to L Tidmarsh	24
	Paid L Tidmarsh amount due to date, by cheque	
3	M Porcher returned goods	48
	M Porcher paid balance due on 1 June 19— by cheque less 3% cash discount	
4	Bought goods on credit from A Waters	125
7	Bought stationery for own office use from L Tidmarsh	120
	Sold goods on credit to S Seaman	150

You are required to write up the personal accounts and the Stationery Account as they would appear in R Wilson's ledger. Sales, Purchases and Returns Accounts are not needed.

To obtain full marks the personal accounts should be written up in three column form: debit, credit and balance.   (*RSA BKI*)

6.2 Payments to the bank

The first job of the day in any business is to open and sort the mail and at Faulkners a special procedure is adopted for dealing with any remittances received in the post. These are recorded in a remittances book and signed for as they are handed over to the cashier. The cashier lists them in the Cash Receipts Journal, making absolutely sure that the cheques are in order. The following points are checked:

1 The cheques all have current dates.
2 The amounts in words and figures are the same.
3 The payee's name, ie P Faulkner & Sons is correct.
4 The cheques are signed.
5 Any alterations on the cheques are clear and are signed.

If a cheque has not been crossed it is the policy of the firm to cross it with two parallel lines before paying it into the bank. When this has been done the remittances are checked carefully with the Cash Receipts Journal. The use of a print calculator simplifies this work as a tally roll is supplied and the total calculated automatically.

A paying-in slip is used for paying the cheques and cash into the firm's Bank Account. Fig 41 on p 78 is an illustration of the paying-in slip for the cheques received on 8 August, ie a total of £16 666.53, as listed in the Cash Receipts Journal on p 59. As Faulkners often have as many as 40 cheques in one day, they supply a copy of the Cash Receipts Journal to the bank to save having to repeat the names of the customers on the paying-in slip.

When there are only four or five cheques these are listed in the column headed 'Cheques, etc' on the reverse of the paying-in slip. On occasions cash and postal orders are received for sales and, as with cheques, these must also be banked on the same day as they are received. An example of a paying-in slip with cheques and cash is shown on p 78 (Fig 42). It was compiled from the following remittances received by P Faulkner & Sons on 9 August 19—.

Coins: 57 @ 1p; 20 @ 2p; 17 @ 5p; 7 @ 10p; 23 @ 50p
Notes: 37 @ £1; 20 @ £5; 3 @ £10; 1 @ £20
Cheques: £7.90 (J Andrews); £21.79 (Bailey Bros); £436.23 (Carters Sports) and £43.10 (Dunn Ltd)

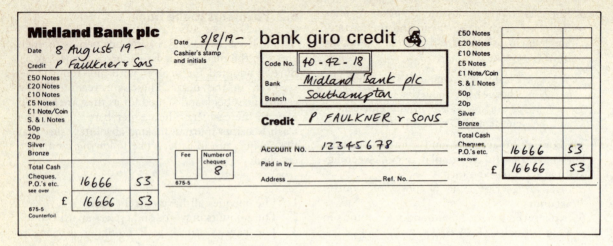

Fig 41   Paying-in slip

Fig 42   Paying-in slip listing cheques and cash

Exercises

1 Enter the cheques recorded in the Cash Receipts Journal for September 3 of Exercise **5**, Section 5.4 (p 61) in a paying-in slip ready for payment into the bank.

2 Complete a paying-in slip for Marion Chadwick of 279 Carter Road, Stannington, Sheffield, to cover the following items paid in today:

5	£5 notes	Cheques for:
21	£1 notes	£38.46
7	50p coins	£11.78
3	10p coins	
5	5p coins	
4	1p coins	
6	½p coins	*(RSA OPI)*

3 *a* The morning post contains the following remittances:

Sender	Method of payment	Amount £
J Smith Ltd	Cheque	4.63
R Peters	Cheque	6.50
P South & Co	Cheque	5.60
M Rayner	PO	1.50
R Jones	Registered mail (five £1 notes)	5.00
The Albright Co Ltd	Cheque	41.31
R Smith	Cheque	4.48

In addition, the following payments are made in cash at the main office:

Paid by:	Money paid:
J Brown	Three £1 notes, two 10p coins and one 5p coin
R Smith	One £5 note, two £1 notes, one 50p coin, two 5p coins and four pennies
S Wilson	One £5 note, and four 10p coins.

Prepare a paying-in slip for all the above receipts to be paid into the bank. The company for whom you work is Western Designs Ltd. Their account number is 1093706. *(RSA OPII)*

6.3 Bank statement and bank reconciliation

At the end of August the bank sent a statement to P Faulkner & Sons giving the firm details of its bank transactions for the month. This statement, received on 2 September, is not like the statements prepared for customers which are reminders of payments due, but is a document showing the state of the firm's account in the bank's books (see p 81). It contains the balance of the account at the beginning of the month (£1 701.00 Cr); credits for the money paid into the bank; debits for money paid out by the bank in accordance with the instructions contained in Faulkner's cheques; debits for any bank charges and the closing balance of £9 328.30 Cr. The bank statement on 2 September is compared and checked with the firm's bank account (p 75). It will be observed that the entries and the balances are the opposite way round to the bank account in the firm's books; the receipts of £1 500 on 1 August were debited in the bank account and credited in the bank statement. This is similar to the situation in the accounts of P Faulkner & Sons and Outdoor Fabrics plc on p 25. The bank, in law, is a person and whereas Faulkners debit their bank account when they pay money in, ie the bank *receives*, in the bank's personal accounts Faulkners must be credited to record the *giving* aspect. There is a difference in the actual figures of the closing balances; the bank account balance before the additions entered under 31 August is £11 938.30 while the bank statement balance is £9 328.30. There are several reasons for this, the main ones being:

1 At any particular time there are cheques which Faulkners have paid that the bank does not know about because:

a the cheque is in the post and the customer has not received it, or

b the customer has received the cheque but has not paid it into his account at his bank, or

c the cheque has been paid into his bank by the customer but it has not been 'cleared', ie it has not been processed by the bank's clearing house and it has not arrived at Faulkner's bank to be entered in the firm's account

2 Faulkners often receive orders and cheques at exhibitions in different parts of the country. The cheques are paid into the nearest bank, by credit transfer, to be credited to the firm's bank at Southampton, but this takes a day or so; those received at the London Exhibition on 31 August (CR49 = £4 000) cannot, therefore, be credited to the Southampton branch until September, which is too late for the bank to record them in its August statement. On the other hand, the firm receives prompt notification of remittances received as the salesmen, with the aid of the secretarial staff at the exhibition, telex to the head office at Southampton details of all orders and remittances received. This information is 'documented' immediately, including the entry in the bank account for the current month of August.

3 The credit transfer system is also used by some customers, who prefer this system instead of cheques. Credit transfers are sent direct to the bank for crediting in the firm's bank account and an advice is sent by the bank to the firm which is used to debit the bank account in the usual way. When credit transfers are received towards the end of the month they will appear on the bank statement, but as the advice has not been received by the firm, they will not have been entered in the firm's bank account. They should, however, be entered in the bank account in the month in which they are actually received by the bank.

4 Occasionally payments are made by standing orders, ie the bank carries out instructions by its customers to pay someone a stated amount on an agreed date. This method of payment is suitable for regular payments of the same amount such as subscriptions or insurance premiums. Faulkners had entered into a hire-purchase agreement with the Regal Machine Company for the purchase of 10 industrial sewing machines involving a payment of £300 at the end of every three months. Holidays or weekends sometimes coincided with the due date and on these occasions the bank made the payment on the first working day in the next month. In any event Faulkners did not know for sure if the payment had been made until the bank statement was received, unless the bank was asked. (*Note* A direct debit has exactly the same effect; the only difference being that the money is paid out on the creditors' instructions.)

5 The bank makes a charge for its services and takes the money out of the firm's account at the end of the month. It debits the amount charged to the firm's account to record the service that the firm has received. As Faulkners do not know what this charge will be, it cannot be entered in the bank account until the statement is received, ie the bank account is left open and entered up from the bank statement as at 31 August.

These factors account for the different figures to be found in the bank statement and the firm's bank account. A bank reconciliation statement (see p 81) is drawn up to check the accuracy of the bank statement with the firm's bank account.

Procedure for preparing a bank reconciliation statement

1 Check both opening balances – in this case bank account £1 701.00 debit = bank statement £1 701.00 credit is correct. If the opening balances are different it will have been 'reconciled' in the previous bank reconciliation statement. It may be necessary, however, to examine the previous statement to check if any differences then are still outstanding.

2 Check the debit column of the bank account with the credit column of the bank statement. In this case all the items appear in both places except the £4 000 in the bank account on 31 August which the bank had not received. It is necessary to make a note of this for inclusion in the bank reconciliation statement as an *addition* to the balance of the bank statement.

3 Check the credit column of the Cash Book, using the Cash Payments Journal for the cheque numbers, with the debit column of the bank statement. The bank statement usually only shows the last three figures of the cheque numbers and not the names of the payees. It is seen that:

   a Cheques numbered 746 and 747 = £1 200 paid on 1 August
   b Cheques numbered 749, 748 and 750 = £6 000 paid on 8 August
   c Of the £610 paid on 20 August only the £27 and £503 appear on the bank statement; the cheques for Kalamazoo (£46) and Barden & Co (£34) have not been received by the bank. These must be noted as a *deduction* in the bank reconciliation statement under the heading of 'Cheques drawn but not presented'

d The Cash Payments Journal on 29 August reveals two cheques drawn – 755 and 756 for £4 000 and £1 620 respectively (credited in the bank account as £5 620) but only the £4 000 cheque appeared on the bank statement. The £1 620 cheque must, therefore, be noted as a *deduction* in the bank reconciliation statement

4   Examine the bank statement for any other items which have not been included in the bank account. It is seen that:

a Bank charges of £10 are included on the bank statement but not in the bank account. This item must be entered in the bank account so that the true balance at the bank is recorded at the end of August.

b There is a standing order of £300 payable to the Regal Machine Co which is also not included in the bank account but has been debited in the bank statement. This is treated in the same way as in *a*.

5   Prepare the bank reconciliation statement, as shown opposite using the following rules (use the bank statement balance as the starting point):

Add money paid in but not credited
Deduct unpresented cheques
Balance = bank account balance

If the balance on the bank statement has Dr following it this means that the account is overdrawn, that is more money has been spent than there is in the account. Most businesses have permission to overdraw but only up to an agreed amount. An overdraft in a bank statement would be shown as a minus figure in a bank reconciliation statement.

If the final balance of the bank reconciliation statement agrees with the bank account balance, P Faulkner & Sons will be satisfied that both records are correct.

MIDLAND BANK PLC		STATEMENT OF ACCOUNT		
Southampton		31 August 19—		
Name: P Faulkner & Sons				

Date 19—	Details	Debit £	Credit £	Balance £
Aug 1	Balance b/f			1701.00 Cr
1	Sundries		1500.00	3201.00 Cr
3	746	500.00		2701.00 Cr
4	747	700.00		2001.00 Cr
8	Sundries		16666.53	18667.53 Cr
11	749	2377.00		16290.53 Cr
12	748	1211.34		15079.19 Cr
12	750	2411.66		12667.53 Cr
15	Sundries		1500.77	14168.30 Cr
25	751	27.00		14141.30 Cr
25	752	503.00		13638.30 Cr
31	755	4000.00		9638.30 Cr
31	Bank charges	10.00		9628.30 Cr
31	S/O	300.00		9328.30 Cr

Bank reconciliation statement at 31 August 19—

	£	£
Balance as per bank statement		9 328.30
Add Money paid in but not credited (CR49)		4 000.00
		13 328.30
Deduct Unpresented cheques:		
Kalamazoo cheque No. 753	46.00	
Bardon & Co 754	34.00	
A Customer 756	1 620.00	
		1 700.00
Balance as per bank account		11 628.30

Amended bank account

	£	£
Balance as at 31 August		11 938.30
Less		
Bank charges entered 2 September	10.00	
Standing order but dated 31 August	300.00	
		310.00
		11 628.30

Exercises

1 It is the usual practice for a businessman to receive a statement from his bank at the end of each month. This statement is then compared with the bank columns of the Cash Book in order to extract a bank reconciliation statement. Below is a bank statement for the month of June 19— and an extract from the Cash Book (bank columns only) for the same month.

By comparison of the two records you are asked to extract the necessary information so as to construct a bank reconciliation statement as at 30 June 19—.

MIDWEST BANK LTD				Account Number	21/368

Mr I N Hand

19—		Debit £	Credit £	Balance £	
June 1	Balance b/f			468.90	Cr
5	Cash and cheques		392.83	861.73	Cr
12	Farmer	129.76		731.97	Cr
14	Cash and cheques		198.83	930.80	Cr
20	Butcher	63.15		867.65	Cr
27	Credit transfer - Jones		100.00	967.65	Cr
28	Standing order – Subscription	20.00		947.65	Cr
28	Bank charges	15.00		932.65	Cr

Cash Book of I N Hand

19—		Debit £	Credit £	Balance £
June 1	Balance b/d			468.90 (Dr)
5	Cash	392.83		861.73
6	Farmer		129.76	731.97
10	Butcher		63.15	668.82
14	Cash	198.83		867.65
20	Baker		292.22	575.43
26	Burdon		77.69	497.74
29	Cash	204.66		702.40

2 The Bank Account of V White and his bank statement received on 31 March 19— are given below:

19—		Debit £	Credit £	Balance £	
March 1	Balance			150.00	Cr
6	Cash		75.00	225.00	Cr
10	A Roe	30.00		195.00	Cr
13	W Wing		17.00	212.00	Cr
15	Credit transfer – B Egg		16.00	228.00	Cr
18	T Salmon	15.00		213.00	Cr
31	Charges	10.00		203.00	Cr

19—		Debit £	Credit £	Balance £	
March 1	Balance b/f			150.00 (Dr)	
6	Cash	75.00		225.00	
8	A Roe		30.00	195.00	
13	W Wing	17.00		212.00	
16	T Salmon		15.00	197.00	
28	R Bird		29.00	168.00	
31	R Nest	39.00		207.00	

You are required to:

a Bring the bank account up to date, and state the new balance at 31 March 19—.

b Prepare a statement, under its proper title, to reconcile the difference between the new up-to-date balance in the bank account and the balance in the bank statement on 31 March 19—. (*University of Cambridge Local Examinations 'O' Level – amended for bank account only*)

3 On 31 May the debit balance on Carr's bank account as shown in the Cash Book was £370.41. The bank statement at that date showed a credit balance of £409.10.

On checking the bank statement against the Cash Book the following differences were found:

a Interest due on a county council loan £36.15 had been collected by the bank but not entered in the Cash Book.

b A standing order £12.17 payable for fire insurance had been paid by the bank but not entered in the Cash Book.

c Cheques amounting to £100.41 entered in the Cash Book had not been presented for payment.

d On 31 May a cheque for £85.70 had been entered in the Cash Book and paid into the bank after the bank statement had been collected from the bank.

Show your calculation of the balance that should appear in the Cash Book and then prepare a bank reconciliation statement.

(*AEB GCE 'O' Level – adapted*)

4 From the following draw up a bank reconciliation statement:

	£
Cash at bank as per bank account	678.00
Unpresented cheques	256.00
Cheques received and paid into the bank but not yet entered on the bank statement	115.00
Credit transfers entered as banked on the bank statement but not entered in the Cash Book	56.00
Cash at bank as per bank statement	875.00

5 William Tanner received the following bank statement on 31 May 19—:

19—		Debit £	Credit £	Balance £
May 1	Balance			332
7	110119	102		230
11	Cash		518	748
18	Credit transfer investment dividends		600	1 348
19	110121	340		1 008
26	Direct debit insurance	78		930

William Tanner checked the statement against his cheque counterfoils and found that cheques numbered 110118 for £235 and 110120 for £136 had not been presented.

The names of the payees of the cheques are:

110118	S Lyle
110119	N Faldo
110120	C O'Connor
110121	K Brown

As William Tanner has not written up his Cash Book for the month of May 19— you are required to:
a write up the bank columns for that month
b balance the bank columns, and reconcile that balance with the amount shown on the bank statement at the end of the month (*RSA BKI*)

6 On 28 February 19— the bank column of W Payne's Cash Book showed a debit balance of £600.

A bank statement written up to 28 February 19— disclosed that the following items had not been entered in the Cash Book:
a the sum of £1 500 received from P Jones by credit transfer
b the transfer of £1 000 from Payne's private bank deposit account into his business bank account
c bank charges £180

When the bank statement was further checked against the Cash Book the following items were discovered:
a cheques drawn in favour of creditors totalling £8 300 had not yet been presented
b cash and cheques £4 100 had been entered in the Cash Book but not yet credited by the bank
c a cheque for £50 drawn by W Payne in respect of drawings had been correctly entered in the Cash Book but debited twice in the bank statement

You are required to prepare as at 28 February 19—:
a A statement showing the adjusted Cash Book balance.
b A bank reconciliation statement showing the balance appearing in the bank statement. (*RSA BKI*)

7 The bank columns of your Cash Book for the month of February 19— are shown below:

19—		£				Cheque No	£
Feb 1	Balance	480	Feb 4	Wages		335	180
22	A Ball	250	5	F Lowe		336	60
22	C Lamb	136	11	G Dow		337	110
22	E Mann	208		J Iles		338	244
26	L Day	85	23	K Peel		339	401
			28	Balance			164
		1 159					1 159
Mar 1	Balance	164					

The following bank statement was received for the month of February:

19–		Dr	Cr	Balance
		£	£	£
Feb 1	Balance			600
3	Cheque No 334	120		480
8	335	180		300
16	338	244		56
17	336	60		4 o/d
23	Sundries		594	590
26	D May credit transfer		65	655
	Ace Insurance standing order	26		
	Charges	18		611

a Make the necessary entries in the cash book and ascertain the correct balance as on 28 February 19—.

b Reconcile your revised Cash Book balance with the balance shown in the bank statement. (*RSA BKI*)

6.4 Petty cash

It is the practice of Faulkners to pay all money received into the bank and all payments over £10 have to be made by cheque. There are, however, many items of less than £10 which a business has to pay for at regular intervals, such as window cleaning, small items of stationery (pens, pencils, postcards, etc) and tea and coffee. These small payments are paid in cash and entered in a Petty Cash Book with columns to analyse the expenditure before posting it to the expense accounts in the Nominal Ledger.

The advantages of using a Petty Cash Book are:

1 Many small items are grouped together under main headings such as stationery or travelling expenses and only the total is posted to the ledger, thus reducing the number of postings.
2 The Bank Account (or Cash Account if one is used) is not filled up with these small items.
3 It allows the work of handling small items of cash to be delegated to a petty cashier and leaves the chief cashier to deal with larger items.

Faulkners use the 'Imprest' system of recording petty cash which has the following features:

1 The imprest (or float) at Faulkners is £50. It has been estimated to be sufficient to cover the petty cash expenditure for one month and is the amount which the petty cashier has in his cash box to start the month.
2 During the month payments are made from the imprest of £50. All expenditure must be covered by a petty cash voucher (Fig 43) or a receipt. This voucher must be signed by the person receiving the money and authorised by a responsible official such as the chief cashier. The vouchers and receipts are numbered and filed numerically for audit purposes.
3 At the end of the month the petty cashier receives a sum of money from the cashier to reimburse him for the amount spent. The system is designed to give control of petty cash expenditure because the size of the balance (the imprest) is fixed at the beginning of the period and can never be more than that. If the imprest is £50 and at the end of the month there is £11 left, the petty cashier receives cash for £39 to restore the imprest.

Fig 43   Petty cash voucher

4 The petty cash can be checked *at any time*, even if the Petty Cash Book is not up to date because:

Petty cash vouchers + Cash held = Imprest

There was £10.50 in the petty cash box on 1 October, so the petty cashier was given a cheque for £39.50 to cash to make up the 'imprest' to £50. During October the following payments were made after being confirmed by petty cash vouchers:

19—		Amount £	VAT (included) £
Oct 3	Cleaning materials	1.65	0.21
8	Bus fare to Winchester	1.37	
9	Biros and pencils	3.25	0.42
10	Tea and sugar	1.50	
10	Milk	1.20	
14	First aid kit for office	6.85	0.89
17	Small bottle aspirins	0.40	0.05
19	Newspapers	2.20	
21	Window cleaning	6.70	0.87
23	Large manilla envelopes	1.43	0.18
28	Donation to Salvation Army	0.50	
31	Bus fare to Mayflower Park Exhibition	0.43	

Dr   Cr

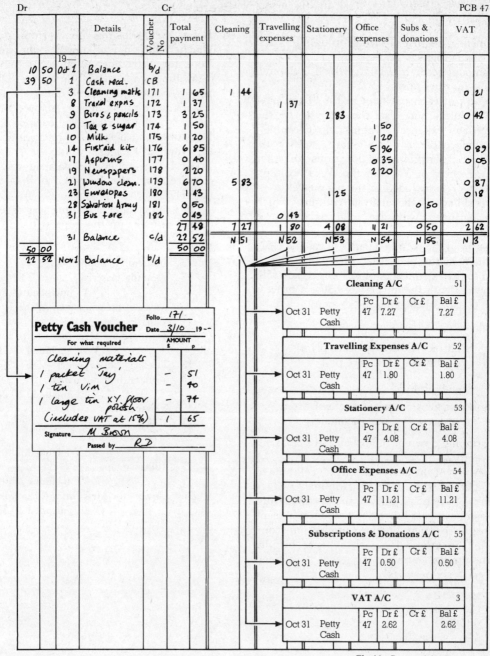

			Details	Voucher No	Total payment		Cleaning		Travelling expenses		Stationery		Office expenses		Subs & donations		VAT	
		19—																
10	50	Oct 1	Balance	b/d														
39	50	1	Cash recd.	CB														
		3	Cleaning matls	171	1	65	1	44									0	21
		8	Travel expns	172	1	37			1	37								
		9	Biros & pencils	173	3	25					2	83					0	42
		10	Tea & sugar	174	1	50							1	50				
		10	Milk	175	1	20							1	20				
		14	First aid kit	176	6	85							5	96			0	89
		17	Aspirins	177	0	40							0	35			0	05
		19	Newspapers	178	2	20							2	20				
		21	Window clean.	179	6	70	5	83									0	87
		23	Envelopes	180	1	43					1	25					0	18
		28	Salvation Army	181	0	50									0	50		
		31	Bus fare	182	0	43			0	43								
					27	48	7	27	1	80	4	08	11	21	0	50	2	62
		31	Balance	c/d	22	52	N 51		N 52		N 53		N 54		N 55		N 3	
50	00				50	00												
22	52	Nov 1	Balance	b/d														

Petty Cash Voucher   Folio _171_   Date _3/10_ 19--

For what required	AMOUNT £	p
Cleaning materials		
1 packet 'Jay'	—	51
1 tin Vim	—	40
1 large tin XY floor polish	—	74
(includes VAT at 15%)	1	65

Signature _M Brown_
Passed by _RD_

Cleaning A/C   51

			Pc	Dr £	Cr £	Bal £
Oct 31	Petty Cash		47	7.27		7.27

Travelling Expenses A/C   52

			Pc	Dr £	Cr £	Bal £
Oct 31	Petty Cash		47	1.80		1.80

Stationery A/C   53

			Pc	Dr £	Cr £	Bal £
Oct 31	Petty Cash		47	4.08		4.08

Office Expenses A/C   54

			Pc	Dr £	Cr £	Bal £
Oct 31	Petty Cash		47	11.21		11.21

Subscriptions & Donations A/C   55

			Pc	Dr £	Cr £	Bal £
Oct 31	Petty Cash		47	0.50		0.50

VAT A/C   3

			Pc	Dr £	Cr £	Bal £
Oct 31	Petty Cash		47	2.62		2.62

Fig 44   Petty cash book

Fig 44   Petty cash book

The example of a Petty Cash Book in Fig 44 on p 87 illustrates:

1 The opening balance of £10.50 brought forward from September.
2 The amount received £39.50, which is debited to make up the imprest to £50.
3 The entry of each payment in the 'Total payment' column and also the analysis to the appropriate expense columns of 'Cleaning', 'Travelling expenses', 'Stationery', 'Office expenses', 'Subscriptions and donations', together with the entry of VAT in the 'VAT' column where VAT is included in the payment.
4 The totalling of the analysis columns which 'cross balances' with the total payments of £27.48.
5 The entry of the closing balance of cash £22.52, contained in the petty cash box which, when added to the expenditure of £27.48, equals £50, ie it agrees with the imprest of £50 – a process which is called balancing off.

To calculate the balance:

Subtract Total payments from
Imprest (total receipts)

To restore the imprest:

Subtract Closing balance of cash from
Imprest = Total payments

6 The bringing down of the balance of £22.52 on 1 November.
7 The posting of the analysed (credit) columns to the debit of the relevant Nominal Ledger Accounts, which is similar to the postings from the Cash Payments Journal for expenses, except that with the petty cash columns only one posting is required for each expense for the month. In this example 12 items have been reduced to six postings.

Exercises

1 Enter the following items from petty cash vouchers into P Faulkner & Sons' Petty Cash Book for November, analysed into Cleaning, Travelling expenses, Stationery, Office expenses, Subscriptions and donations and VAT. Total the columns, cross balance, balance off on 30 November, bring the balance down on 1 December and post to the relevant accounts in the Nominal Ledger.

On 1 November the balance was brought forward from the Petty Cash Book on p 87 (PCB47).

On 2 November a cheque was received and cashed to make up the imprest to £50.

19—		£
Nov 3	Donation to Poppy Day	0.50
3	Cleaning materials (VAT included £1.50)	11.50
6	Advertisement for staff in the 'Guardian'	7.75
9	Taxi fare for Miss Jones (ill) (VAT included £0.20)	1.55
13	Tea bags, coffee, sugar – 2 lb	2.87
14	6 rulers, blotting paper (VAT included £0.28)	2.20
19	Newspapers	2.30
23	Milk	1.12
24	Scissors for office (VAT included £0.05)	0.44
25	Adhesive tape (VAT included £0.04)	0.36
30	Flowers for Miss Jones (ill in hospital) (VAT included £0.37)	2.87

2 A Petty Cash Book is kept on the imprest system, the amount of the imprest being £50.00.

Give the ruling for the book, providing suitable columns and enter the following transactions:

			VAT included £
19—			
Nov 1	Balance in hand of petty cashier £16.40		
1	Cash received from chief cashier restoring the imprest		
2	Cash purchases £7.45		0.97
3	Paid sundry travelling expenses £2.50		—
6	Purchased stationery £6.10		0.79
7	Cleaners wages £7.00		—
8	Repairs to typewriter £5.50		0.72
8	Bought postage stamps £3.00		—
9	Office tea and sugar £2.50		—
10	Typewriter ribbons £4.20		0.55

Balance the book on 10 November and total the analysis columns. (*RSA BKI*)

3 The Petty Cash Book below contains a number of errors. Rewrite the book in a correct manner and comment on the effect of the errors.

4 Greaves (Builders) Ltd keep their petty cash on the imprest system with a £60 float and analyse its expenditure into: stationery, travelling expenses, telephone expenses, miscellaneous expenses, and deductible input tax (this last item is to record the VAT element in any expenses paid through petty cash).

Enter up the Petty Cash Book from the following details, balance off at the end of the month, restore the imprest on 1 July, and state where the items would be posted to in the ledger.

19—		£
June 1	Balance in hand (float)	60.00
2	Paid for envelopes (VAT included £0.28)	2.20
3	Paid travelling expenses	5.00
5	Paid telephone expenses (VAT included £3.00)	23.00
8	Bought first aid kit (VAT included £0.71)	5.50
10	Paid for biros (VAT included £0.03)	0.22
16	Paid travelling expenses	7.00
22	Bought string (VAT included £0.07)	0.55
23	Paid for tea, milk & sugar	3.00
25	Bought 2 tins glue (for use on buildings) (VAT included £0.32)	2.47
30	Paid cleaner	5.00
30	Paid for cleaning materials (VAT included £0.12)	0.99

Receipts		Date	Details	Voucher /Folio No.	Total payments		Motor expenses		Office expenses		Postage		Purchases		Travelling expenses		VAT	
		19—																
7	37	JAN 1	Balance	b/f														
92	63	2	Cash rec'd	8														
		3	Petrol & oil	1	7	63									6	64	—	99
		4	Stationery	2	3	21			2	79							—	42
		5	Postage stamps	3	3	12					3	21						
		10	Travel exes	4	6	43							6	34				
		13	Envelopes	5	4	51					3	92					—	59
		18	Window cleaning	6	2 30				2	—							—	30
		24	Salesmens															
			Driving licence	7	5	—									5	—		
		28	Cleaners wages	8	25	—			25	—								
		30	Trade samples	9	12	10							10	53			1	57
			Initial towel	10	7 70	X 1	00										X 6	70
					77	00	1	00	29	79	7	13	16	87	11	64	10	57
		30	Balance	c/d	23	00												
100	—				100													
32	—	Feb 1	Balance	b/d														
68	—	2	Cash rec'd	CB														

5 Alfred Robertson pays all receipts into the bank and makes all cash payments out of petty cash. At the end of each week the petty cashier is given a cheque to restore the imprest.

At the close of business on 18 April 19— Robertson's bank balance according to his Cash Book was £935.75, and his cash in hand stood at the imprest amount of £50.

The counterfoils of his paying in book for the next week showed:

April 20	Total paid in £308.65 consisting of cash from sales £250.15 and a cheque from D Preston for £58.50 in full settlement of £60 owed by him
22	Total paid in £260.90 consisting of a cheque from F Ives of £22.75 and £238.15 cash from sales
24	Total paid in £210 consisting entirely of cash from sales

The counterfoils of his cheque book show:

April 21	Midlands Electricity Board for lighting	£165.92
22	G Lamb & Son in settlement of £100 owing to them	£95.00
25	Petty cash	£29.50
	Self	£50.00

Payments out of petty cash were as follows:

April 20	Paid cleaner	£8.00
22	Postage stamps	£2.90
24	Stationery	£7.00
24	Cleaning materials	£3.00
25	Travelling expenses	£3.00
25	Letterheaded paper	£5.60

You are required to write up

a the Bank Cash Book (The detail columns of the Bank Cash Book should indicate clearly which ledger account is to be debited or credited in respect of each entry.)

b the Petty Cash Book with analysis columns for cleaning, postages, travelling and stationery. (*RSA BKI*)

7 The Journal

From your study of accounts up to this stage you will have observed that Faulkners have made provision for recording the transactions shown in the chart below. There are, however, several kinds of transactions which do not come under any of these four headings and these include:

1 Entries to open a set of ledgers
2 The purchase or sale on credit of capital items, ie those relating to capital expenditure – see p 93
3 Writing off bad debts
4 Correction of errors
5 Writing off expense accounts
6 Recording depreciation (ie assets losing value)

In order to authorise these transactions for entry into the ledger, another 'book of original entry' called the Journal acts as a diary to record their details. It is significant that with the introduction of the computer, Journal transfers are obligatory.

7.1 Opening entries

When Mr P Faulkner started his business he did not keep a full set of double-entry books. After a number of years in business, as the business grew, it became essential for him to have a proper system to deal with the volume of transactions and so the Journal was used to do this. At that time he had:

Money in the bank £423
Cash in hand £50
Stock of goods and materials which cost £1 200
Machinery and equipment worth £250
Two customers, Mr Parkway and Mr Fothergill owed him £220 and £73 respectively, whilst he owed £216 to Mr Gillforth for goods supplied.

The things he possessed, which are called assets, added up to £2 216 (ie £423 + £50 + £1 200 + £250 + £220 + £73).

He had only one amount owing, which is called a liability, of £216. The value of the business, known as capital, is calculated as follows:

	£
Assets	2 216
Less Liabilities	216
= Capital	2 000

	Purchases	Sales	Returns		Money	
	On Credit	On Credit	In	Out	In	Out
Source of information	Supplier's invoice	Copy of Faulkner's sales invoice	Copy of Faulkner's credit note	Supplier's credit note	Cheques/ Cash Receipts Journal	Cheques/ Cash Payments Journal Vouchers
Entered in Day Book	Purchases Journal	Sales Journal	Sales Returns Journal	Purchases Returns Journal	Cash Book/ Bank Account	Cash Book/ Bank Account Petty Cash Book
Posted to ledger accounts Dr	Purchases	Customer	Sales returns	Supplier	Bank	Supplier/Expense
Cr	Supplier	Sales	Customer	Purchases returns	Customer	Bank/Petty cash

The layout of the Journal is as follows:

Date	Details	Fo	Dr	Cr
	The name(s) of the account(s) to be debited		x x	
	Followed by the name(s) of the account(s) to be credited – including Capital Account			x x x
	An explanation of the entry called the narrative			

Mr P Faulkner was optimistic about his business prospects and allowed for expansion by using separate ledgers for:

	using code numbers:
Impersonal accounts – Nominal Ledger	1–99
Customers accounts – Sales Ledger	100–199
Suppliers accounts – Purchases Ledger	200–299

The following illustrates the postings from the Journal to the ledger accounts:

Opening Journal Entries for P Faulkner with postings to the ledger accounts

				J1
Date 19—	Details	Fo	Dr £	Cr £
April 1	Bank Account Dr	CB1	423.00	
	Cash Account Dr	CB1	50.00	
	Stock Account Dr	NL1	1200.00	
	Machinery & Equipment Account Dr	NL2	250.00	
	M Parkway Account Dr	SL100	220.00	
	C Fothergill Dr	SL101	73.00	
	M Gillforth Account	PL200		216.00
	Capital Account	NL3		2000.00
	Assets, liabilities and capital to open the books.		2216.00	2216.00

Dr					**Cash Book**				Cr
19—	Details	Fo	Cash £	Bank £	19—	Details	Fo	Cash £	Bank £
April 1	Balances	J1	50.00	423.00					

Nominal Ledger

	Stock Account				NL1
19--	Details	Fo	Dr £	Cr £	Bal £
Apr 1	Balance	J1	1200.00		1200.00

	Machinery and Equipment Account				NL2
19--	Details	Fo	Dr £	Cr £	Bal £
Apr 1	Balance	J1	250.00		250.00

	Capital Account				NL3
19--	Details	Fo	Dr £	Cr £	Bal £
Apr 1	Balance	J1		2000.00	2000.00 Cr

Sales Ledger

	M Parkway Account				SL100
19--	Details	Fo	Dr £	Cr £	Bal £
Apr 1	Balance	J1	220.00		220.00

	C Fothergill Account				SL101
19--	Details	Fo	Dr £	Cr £	Bal £
Apr 1	Balance	J1	73.00		73.00

Purchases Ledger

	M Gillforth Account				PL200
19--	Details	Fo	Dr £	Cr £	Bal £
Apr 1	Balance	J1		216.00	216.00 Cr

7.2 Purchase and sale on credit of capital items

P Faulkner purchased on credit a second-hand van for £1 200 from The Trelawne Motor Company to be paid for in instalments of £100 per month.

The Journal entry and posting to ledger accounts are as follows:

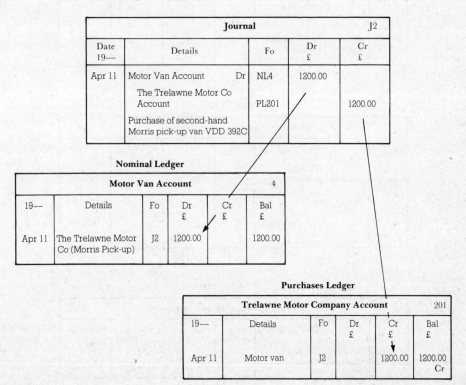

Journal				J2
Date 19---	Details	Fo	Dr £	Cr £
Apr 11	Motor Van Account Dr	NL4	1200.00	
	The Trelawne Motor Co Account	PL201		1200.00
	Purchase of second-hand Morris pick-up van VDD 392C			

Nominal Ledger

	Motor Van Account				4
19--	Details	Fo	Dr £	Cr £	Bal £
Apr 11	The Trelawne Motor Co (Morris Pick-up)	J2	1200.00		1200.00

Purchases Ledger

	Trelawne Motor Company Account				201
19---	Details	Fo	Dr £	Cr £	Bal £
Apr 11	Motor van	J2		1200.00	1200.00 Cr

Although the van is bought it is not the usual 'purchases' which only contain those goods which are bought for resale. The van is an asset (still to be paid for) and The Trelawne Motor Company, a liability of Faulkners, which is put with the other creditors for convenience.

On 15 April P Faulkner sold an old typewriter to Anne Teeke for £30 on credit which was the price he had paid for it. This had been entered as part of the £250 in the Machinery and Equipment Account. On the following day P Faulkner bought an electric typewriter on credit for £200 from Skipton Office Equipment Company. The Journal and Ledger entries using the existing accounts are:

Journal				J3
Date 19—	Details	Fo	Dr £	Cr £

Apr 15	Anne Teeke Dr
	  Machinery and
	  Equipment Account
	  Sale of Imperial typewriter
		SL 102
		NL2
			30.00	30.00

Apr 16	Machinery and Equipment
	Account Dr
	  Skipton Office
	  Equipment Company
	  Account
	
	  Purchase of Triumph
	  electric typewriter
		NL2
		
		SL202
			200.00	200.00

Sales Ledger

Anne Teeke Account					102
19—	Details	Fo	Dr £	Cr £	Bal £
Apr 15	Machinery and Equipment (Imperial typewriter)	J3	30.00		30.00

Nominal Ledger

Machinery and Equipment Account					2
19—	Details	Fo	Dr £	Cr £	Bal £
Apr 1	Balance	J1	250.00		250.00
15	Anne Teeke	J3		30.00	220.00
16	Skipton Office Equipment Company	J3	200.00		420.00

Purchases Ledger

Skipton Office Equipment Company					202
19—	Details	Fo	Dr £	Cr £	Bal £
Apr 16	Machinery and Equipment (Triumph typewriter)	J3		200.00	200.00 Cr

In these illustrations it will be seen that the asset accounts of the motor van and machinery and equipment were debited to record the receiving of the items whilst the suppliers (although not trade suppliers of goods) were credited to give the 'giving' effect. In a similar manner £30 was recorded to the credit of the machinery and equipment account to indicate that some of the equipment had been sold. It would be incorrect to credit sales account as this account only contains goods sold from the stock-in-trade. The corresponding debit was to the receiver, Anne Teeke.

7.3 Writing off bad debts

The ledger entries for writing off a bad debt of £24 were given on p 58. The Journal entry is:

Journal				J4
Date 19—	Details	Fo	Dr £	Cr £
Aug 31	Bad Debts Account Dr	NL42	24.00	
	I M Credit & Co Account	SL130		24.00
	Debt written off as a bad debt due to failure to contact debtor			

7.4 Correction of errors

Some errors do not affect the arithmetical accuracy of the books whilst others cause the totals of the Trial Balance (Unit 9) to not 'agree'. All of the errors which follow do not affect the agreement of the figures in the Trial Balance and, before amending the errors in the accounts, they must be entered in the Journal (or journalised):

1 The sale of an asset (a typewriter) for £25 credited to sales account.
2 A debit entry in the wrong customer's account for £120, ie A Tonge instead of A Tomb.
3 The purchase of new machinery debited to Purchases Account £2 100.
4 The payment of motor expenses £57 debited to Motor Van Account.
5 Discount allowed debited to Discount Received Account £25.

Can you spot the errors in these transactions?

The Journal entries to correct the errors are:

	Date 19—	Details		Fo	Dr £	Cr £
		Journal				J5
1	Sept 30	Sales Account	Dr		25.00	
		Machinery and Equipment Account				25.00
		Correction of error in posting sale of typewriter to Sales Account				
2	Sept 30	A Tomb Account	Dr		120.00	
		A Tonge Account				120.00
		Correction of error in debiting A Tonge instead of A Tomb				
3	Sept 30	Machinery & Equipment Account	Dr		2100.00	
		Purchases Account				2100.00
		Correction of error in debiting Purchases Account with purchase of new machinery				
4	Sept 30	Motor Expenses Account	Dr		57.00	
		Motor Vans Account				57.00
		Correction of error in debiting Motor Van Account instead of Motor Expenses Account				
5	Sept 30	Discount Allowed Account	Dr		25.00	
		Discount Received Account				25.00
		Correction of error in posting Discount Allowed to Discount Received Account				

Exercises

1 Draft the Journal entries to record or correct the following on June 4 19—:

a A debt owed by T Warren of £270 is to be written off as a bad debt.
b New machinery and plant is purchased from Steel Makers Ltd on credit for £40 000.
c Goods taken by the proprietor value £700 had been debited to an account in the Sales Ledger opened in the proprietor's own name (R Browning).
d A letter had been received from a supplier, P Shelley, stating definitely that £24 cash discount deducted would not be allowed.

(*RSA BKI*)

2 Draft the Journal entries required to record the following in the books of a grocer:

		£
June 3	Purchased on credit, office furniture from Crescent Furniture Manufacturers Ltd	4 500
7	Wrote off Philip Richards account as a bad debt	470
9	Corrected an error in posting; John Bell had been debited in error instead of John Belling	150
10	Sold on credit to Car Traders old motor van at book value	70

Marks will be given for narrations which explain and clarify the entry. (*RSA BKI*)

3 James White on checking his accounting records discovers that he has made the following errors:

   a A filing cabinet recently purchased for £115 had been charged in error to the General Expenses Account.

   b The account of S Blaker had been debited with goods £75 sold to S Blakeman.

   c An amount of £172 for machinery repairs had been debited to the Machinery (Asset) Account.

   d Discounts allowed £27 had been posted to the debit of Discounts Received Account.

   e When paying G Hale his account of £60, cash discount of £3 had been deducted in error. Hale has subsequently disallowed this.

   f A payment of £76 for rates had been debited in error to the Rent Account.

You are required to prepare journal entries in the books of James White to correct the above errors. (*RSA BKI*)

4 Your firm trades in office machinery and on 1 March 19— its financial position was as follows:

	£
Freehold land and buildings	15 000
Cash at bank	12 000
Trade debtors	250
Trade creditors	200
Fixtures and fittings	4 000
Stock on hand	14 000

   a Enter the above in the Journal showing the capital at that date.

   b Enter the following transactions for the month of March in the appropriate day books. All are subject to VAT at 10%.

Mar 1   Sold 4 typewriters to Super Office Services, list price £80 each, allowing them 10% trade discount

    4   Bought 6 calculators from Wye Accessories at £12 each net

   12   Sold a duplicating machine to J Smithers at £350 net

   16   Sold 4 calculators to Markov Ltd list price £20 each allowing them 10% trade discount

   20   Bought 6 typewriters from Acme Products Ltd list price £40 each. We were allowed trade discount of 15%

   25   Sold 2 duplicating machines to Murgatroyds, list price £350, allowing them trade discount of 10%

Note: Entries in the ledger accounts are not required. (*RSA BKI*)

5 During the months of March and April the following transactions took place on Micawber's account in the books of Pickwick.

		£
Mar 1	Micawber owes Pickwick	400
3	Micawber paid the balance on his account by cheque being allowed cash discount of 2½%	
10	Micawber obtained further goods on credit value	250
14	Micawber returned goods to Pickwick value	50
21	Pickwick received cash on account	100
Apr 30	You are informed that Micawber has gone out of business due to financial difficulties, and it is decided to write off the balance on his account as a bad debt	

   a Write up Micawber's account for the months of March and April.

   b Show the entry in the Bad Debts Account caused by the above transactions. (*RSA BKI*)

8 Stock-taking and the Stock Account

Stock-taking has to be carried out regularly by physically counting the stock to check that it agrees with the written records; it is essential that this is done at the end of each year to coincide with the preparation of the Trading Account (see Unit 10).

On 31 March P Faulkner had £200 of stock as shown in the ledger account on p 99. This stock is used during the year and is debited to the Trading Account by means of a journal entry.

At the end of the year stock sheets are prepared by recording:

1 The description, quantity and any special comments after counting each stock item.
2 The cost price and the expected selling price taken from the records in the accounts department.
3 The 'extensions', ie the quantities multiplied by the prices in the relevant columns.
4 The lower of either the cost value or the expected selling value (known as the net realisable value) in the right-hand column.
5 The totals of the three columns: cost value, net realisable value and lower of cost or net realisable value.

The right-hand column, ie the lower of cost or net realisable value is the value used for stock-taking.

The diagram on p 99 shows the procedure for entering stock in the Journal and posting it to the Stock Account.

Exercises

1 Rule up a stock sheet for P Faulkner & Sons at 31 March 19— for completed products. Enter the following items, extend the cost values, enter the net realisable prices, extend the net realisable values and enter the lower of the cost or net realisable value in the last column. Total the three value columns. Refer to the price list on p 39 for the descriptions.

Reference	Quantity	Cost price £	Net realisable price £
774T	28	110.00	90.00
583T	60	70.00	112.00
13SB	80	13.50	16.50
14SB	40	13.00	13.00
15SB	100	12.00	11.50

2 Mayflower Fashion Boutique has the following goods in stock at 31 December. Enter them on to a stock sheet and work out the stock value for the end of the year.

Commodity	Quantity	Cost price £	Net realisable price £
'Patch' jeans	50	14.00	13.00
Smock dresses	40	15.00	14.00
'Ginger Rogers' suits	60	18.00	22.00
Knee length boots	170	18.00	23.00

								Stock at 31 March 19—					

Code No	Details	Special comment	Quantity	Cost price £	Cost value £	Net realis-able price £	Net realis-able value £	Lower of cost or net realisable value £
523T	Expedition		1	108.00	108.00	157.00	157.00	108.00
583T	Hiker	Old Stock	5	70.00	350.00	34.00	170.00	170.00
79C	Resteasy		1	13.00	13.00	15.75	15.75	13.00
79C	Resteasy	Damaged/ shop soiled	3	13.00	39.00	3.00	9.00	9.00
					510.00		351.75	300.00

	Journal				59
Date 19—	Details	Fo	Dr £	Cr £	
March 31	Trading Account　　　Dr	T	200.00		
	Stock Account	NL1		200.00	
	Transfer of opening stock (at 1 April) to Trading Account				
March 31	Stock Account　(1/4/—) Dr	NL1	300.00		
	Trading Account	T		300.00	
	Transfer of stock at end of year from Trading Account as per stock valuation sheet				

	Stock Account				NL1
19—	Details	Fo	Dr £	Cr £	Balance £
19—(1) April 1	Balance	b/f			200.00
19—(2) March 31	Transfer to Trading A/c	J59		200.00	—
April 1	Transfer from Trading A/c	J59	300.00		300.00

3 Enter the following items in a Stock Account, including the entry transferring stock to the Trading Account at 31 March 19— (2):

19— (1) 　1 April 　Opening stock 　£12 000
19— (2) 　31 March 　Closing stock 　£15 000

4 Mr P Faulkner, the Managing Director of P Faulkner & Sons wanted to know urgently the profit for the half-year to 30 September 19—, ie at the end of the camping season, and have an end-of-season sale to make room for the new, next year's range. The stock list opposite was taken out in a hurry and contains a number of errors. Re-write it, making any necessary corrections:

				Stock of completed products at 30 September 19—		
Ref	Quantity	Cost price	Cost value £	Net realisable price £	Net realisable value £	Lower of cost or net realisable value £
734T	70	170.00	11900.00	298.00	20860.00	11900.00
754T	40	140.00	5600.00	136.00	5440.00	5440.00
553T	30	84.00	2520.00	130.00	390.00	390.00
583T	12	70.00	840.00	60.00	720.00	720.00
13SB	20	13.50	250.00	12.00	240.00	250.00
14SB	15	13.00	195.00	14.00	210.00	159.00
			£21305.00		£27860.00	£18859.00

9 The Trial Balance and the Suspense Account

9.1 Trial Balance

At the end of every month it is the normal practice for a business to test the accuracy of its accounts by constructing a Trial Balance. The Trial Balance is a list of balances extracted from all of the cash, bank and ledger accounts on a certain date to see if the total of the debit entries is equal to the total of the credit entries. For every debit value there must be a corresponding credit value and vice versa and it follows that if the entries have been recorded correctly the totals of the Trial Balance should be the same.

The purposes of the Trial Balance are:

a To check the arithmetical accuracy of the entries in the accounts. (This does not, however, guarantee that the accounts are correct as some errors are not revealed by arithmetical means, eg posting car repairs to the Car Account.)

b To provide a basis for calculating the profit (Units 10 and 11) and preparing the Balance Sheet (Unit 12).

In Unit 7 the Journal opening entries were given for P Faulkner together with the ledger entries. At that time he used a basic two-column Cash Book. During the month of April he had the following transactions:

Date 19—	Transaction	Value £	+ VAT £
Apr 1	Balances posted from Journal (J1)		
1	Paid rent by cheque	300.00	
2	Sold goods on credit to M Parkway	160.00	24.00
5	Cashed cheque for business use	50.00	
6	Paid for electricity in cash	57.27	
8	Bought goods on credit from M Gillforth	200.00	30.00
11*	Bought motor van on credit from Trelawne Motor Company	1 200.00	
15*	Sold old typewriter to Anne Teeke on credit	30.00	
16*	Bought new typewriter on credit from Skipton Office Equipment Company	200.00	
20	Sold goods on credit to C Fothergill	100.00	15.00
24	Received two cheques:		
	M Parkway	220.00	
	C Fothergill	73.00	
26	Paid rates by cheque	520.00	
29	Received cash from Southampton Travel Insurance Service for commission (introducing customers)	87.00	
29	Paid cash for deposit for holiday in Switzerland	60.00	
29	Paid cash into the bank	60.00	
30	Paid M Gillforth by cheque	216.00	

Notes:

1 On 5 April Mr Faulkner withdrew money from the bank to use in the business, by cashing a cheque, and on 29 April he paid cash into the Bank Account; both of these are known as **contra** entries because the cash is offset against the bank or vice versa so that in total the cash and bank balances together do not change. A 'C' is put in the folio column to indicate this posting.

2 When money is used for non-business matter, as on 29 April, this is called **drawings** (the personal expenditure of the proprietor) and a Drawings Account is debited.

3 The Journal opening entries and the Journal entries for the items marked * were completed in Unit 7 on pp 92 to 94.

4 When the Trial Balance is constructed the balances are extracted from the accounts. The balance is the amount by which the debit amounts exceed the credit amounts or vice versa and it is entered in the Trial Balance in the appropriate column – Dr for a Dr balance and Cr for a Cr balance.

Dr 19—	Details	Fo	Cash £	Bank £	19—	Details	Fo	Cash £	Cr Bank £
Apr 1	Balances	J1	50.00	423.00	Apr 1	Rent	NL5		300.00
5	Bank	C	50.00		5	Cash	C		50.00
24	M Parkway	SL 100		220.00	6	Electricity	NL7	57.27	
24	C Fothergill	SL 101		73.00	26	Rates	NL6		520.00
29	Commission	NL 8	87.00		29	Drawings	NL9	60.00	
					29	Bank	C	60.00	
29	Cash	C		60.00	30	M Gillforth	PL 200		216.00
30	Balance	c/d		310.00	30	Balance	c/d	9.73	
			187.00	1086.00				187.00	1086.00
May 1	Balance	b/d	9.73		May 1	Balance	b/d		310.00

P Faulkner Cash Book — CB10

Note: The £310.00 credit balance in the bank column on 30 April means that Mr Faulkner has paid out £310.00 more than he has in the bank. This is called an overdraft and requires the bank manager's permission. Mr Faulkner had permission to overdraw by up to £400.

P Faulkner Day Books

	Purchases Book						PB20
Date 19—	Supplier	Inv No	Fo	Total £	Goods £	VAT £
Apr 8	M Gillforth	75	PL200	230.00	200.00	30.00
					NL10	NL12

Sales Book						SB30
Date 19—	Customer	Inv No	Fo	Total £	Goods £	VAT £
Apr 2	M Parkway	213	SL100	184.00	160.00	24.00
20	C Fothergill	214	SL101	115.00	100.00	15.00
				299.00	260.00	39.00
					NL11	NL12

Purchases Ledger

M Gillforth Account					PL.200
19—	Details	Fo	Dr £	Cr £	Bal £
Apr 1	Balance	J1		216.00	216.00
8	Invoice	PB20		230.00	446.00
30	Payment	CB10	216.00		230.00 Cr

Trelawne Motor Company Account					PL.201
19—	Details	Fo	Dr £	Cr £	Bal £
Apr 11	Motor van	J2		1200.00	1200.00 Cr

Skipton Office Equipment Company					PL.202
19—	Details	Fo	Dr £	Cr £	Bal £
Apr 16	Machinery and Equipment (Triumph typewriter).	J3		200.00	200.00 Cr

Sales Ledger

M Parkway Account					SL100
19—	Details	Fo	Dr £	Cr £	Bal £
Apr 1	Balance	J1	220.00		220.00
2	Invoice	SB30	184.00		404.00
24	Payment	CB10		220.00	184.00

C Fothergill Account					SL101
19—	Details	Fo	Dr £	Cr £	Bal £
April 1	Balance	J1	73.00		73.00
20	Invoice	SB30	115.00		188.00
24	Payment	CB10		73.00	115.00

Anne Teeke Account					SL102
19—	Details	Fo	Dr £	Cr £	Bal £
Apr 15	Machinery and Equipment (Imperial typewriter)	J3	30.00		30.00

Nominal Ledger

Stock Account					NL1
19—	Details	Fo	Dr £	Cr £	Bal £
Apr 1	Balance	J1	1200.00		1200.00

Machinery and Equipment Account					NL2
19—	Details	Fo	Dr £	Cr £	Bal £
Apr 1	Balance	J1	250.00		250.00
15	Anne Teeke	J3		30.00	220.00
16	Skipton Office Equipment Company	J3	200.00		420.00

Capital Account					NL3
19—	Details	Fo	Dr £	Cr £	Bal £
Apr 1	Balance	J1		2000.00	2000.00 Cr

Motor Van Account					NL4
19—	Details	Fo	Dr £	Cr £	Bal £
Apr 11	Trelawne Motor Co (Morris Pick-up)	J2	1200.00		1200.00

Rent Account					NL5
19—	Details	Fo	Dr £	Cr £	Bal £
Apr 1	Payment	J2	300.00	CB10	300.00

Rates Account — NL6

19—	Details	Fo	Dr £	Cr £	Bal £
Apr 26	Payment	CB10	520.00		520.00

Lighting and Heating Account — NL7

19—	Details	Fo	Dr £	Cr £	Bal £
Apr 6	Payment	CB10	57.27		57.27

Commission Received Account — NL8

19—	Details	Fo	Dr £	Cr £	Bal £
Apr 29	Payment	CB10		87.00	87.00 Cr

Drawings Account — NL9

19—	Details	Fo	Dr £	Cr £	Bal £
Apr 29	Payment (Holiday deposit)	CB10	60.00		60.00

Purchases Account — NL10

19—	Details	Fo	Dr £	Cr £	Bal £
Apr 30	Total for month	PB20	200.00		200.00

Sales Account — NL11

19—	Details	Fo	Dr £	Cr £	Bal £
Apr 30	Total for month	SB30		260.00	260.00 Cr

VAT Account — NL12

19—	Details	Fo	Dr £	Cr £	Bal £
Apr 30	Purchases	PB20	30.00		30.00
30	Sales	SB30		39.00	9.00 Cr

Trial Balance of P Faulkner as at 30 April 19—

Accounts	Dr £	Cr £
Cash	9.73	
Bank (overdraft)		310.00
M Gillforth		230.00
Trelawne Motor Co		1 200.00
Skipton Office Equipment Co		200.00
M Parkway	184.00	
C Fothergill	115.00	
Anne Teeke	30.00	
Stock (1/4/19—)	1 200.00	
Machinery and equipment	420.00	
Capital		2 000.00
Motor van	1 200.00	
Rent	300.00	
Rates	520.00	
Lighting and heating	57.27	
Commission received		87.00
Drawings	60.00	
Purchases	200.00	
Sales		260.00
VAT		9.00
	4 296.00	4 296.00

9.2 Suspense Account

The Suspense Account may be used temporarily to accommodate the difference when the totals of a Trial Balance are unequal, eg if the credit total is larger than the debit total the difference is placed in a Suspense Account in the debit column.

The following Trial Balance was extracted on 31 December. As can be seen, the totals do not agree.

Trial Balance of B Radford as at 31 December 19—

Accounts	Dr £	Cr £
Capital		7 450.00
Drawings	3 000.00	
Stock (1/1/19—)	2 500.00	
Debtors	2 950.00	
Creditors		2 684.00
Equipment	1 530.00	
Purchases and sales	5 140.00	7 460.00
General expenses	680.00	
Discount received		40.00
Cash at bank	1 660.00	
Purchases returns		40.00
	17 500.00	17 534.00

The following procedure may be used to trace the error(s):

Procedure	Errors disclosed in B Radford's Trial Balance and accounts
1 Add up the Dr and Cr columns of the Trial Balance and check the totals.	The Cr column is £100 short: amend the total to £17 634.
2 Find the difference between the two totals and: *a* search through the ledger accounts for this amount *b* divide this amount by 2 and see if there is an item of the same amount on the wrong side of the Trial Balance	£17 634 − £17 500 = £134 £134 ÷ 2 = £67
3 Check the Trial Balance to see if the items are on the correct sides.	Discount received has been entered in the Dr column – it should be in the Cr column. The difference is now: Cr £17 674.00 − Dr £17 460 = £214
4 At this stage a Suspense Account may be opened in the Nominal Ledger with a debit balance to represent the difference between the two totals.	Enter a balance of £214 in the Dr column.
5 Check the extraction of the figures from the ledger accounts to the Trial Balance.	General expenses should be £860 (not £680). Complete the Journal and post to: General Expenses A/c Dr £180 Suspense A/c Cr £180
6 Check the totals of the Day Books.	The Sales Book goods column was undercast (ie added up too little) by £100. Complete the Journal and post to: Suspense A/c Dr £100 Sales A/c Cr £100
7 Check that folio numbers have been entered as an omission may indicate that a transaction has not been posted to a ledger account.	A sales invoice of £150 entered in the Sales Day Book in December was not posted to the customer's account. Complete the Journal and post to: Customer A/c Dr £150 Suspense A/c Cr £150 Also bank deposit interest of £16 had not been posted from the Cash Book. Complete the Journal and post to: Suspense A/c Dr £16 Interest Received A/c Cr £16 Once the balance in the Suspense Account has been removed, as in this case, it suggests that the errors have been found and corrected and an amended Trial Balance can be drawn up.

The journal entries, Suspense Account and amended Trial Balance for the above transactions are given on p 106.

Journal				J6
Date 19——	Details	Fo	Dr £	Cr £
Dec 31	General Expenses Account Dr		180.00	
	Suspense Account			180.00
	Correction of error in posting wrong amount to General Expenses Account			
Dec 31	Suspense Account Dr		100.00	
	Sales Account			100.00
	Correction of error in undercasting Sales Book total			
Dec 31	Customer Account Dr		150.00	
	Suspense Account			150.00
	Correction of error in failing to post invoice to Customer's Account			
Dec 31	Suspense Account Dr		16.00	
	Interest Received Account			16.00
	Correction of error in failing to post bank deposit interest from the Cash Book			

Suspense Account						NL 13
19–	Details	Fo	Dr £	Cr £		Bal £
Dec 31	Balance	TB	214.00			214.00 Dr
31	General expenses			180.00		34.00 Dr
31	Sales		100.00			134.00 Dr
31	Customer			150.00		16.00 Cr
31	Interest received		16.00			–

Amended Trial Balance of B Radford as at 31 December 19–

Accounts	Dr £	Cr £
Capital		7 450.00
Drawings	3 000.00	
Stock (1/1/19—)	2 500.00	
Debtors	3 100.00	
Creditors		2 684.00
Equipment	1 530.00	
Purchases and sales	5 140.00	7 560.00
General expenses	860.00	
Discount received		40.00
Cash at bank	1 660.00	
Purchases returns		40.00
Interest received		16.00
	17 790.00	17 790.00

Exercises

1 E Parsons started business as a dealer in musical instruments on 1 April; he paid £8 000 into the business Bank Account. Enter this amount into the accounts by debiting the Bank Account and crediting the Capital Account.

Record the following transactions for April, opening new accounts where necessary, and take out a Trial Balance on 30 April:

		£
April 4	Bought new instruments on credit (ie purchases) – including £450 VAT	3 450
8	Sales on credit – including £75 VAT	575
15	Sales on credit – including £240 VAT	1 840
24	Paid creditors by cheques	2 000
30	Received cheques from debtors	500

2 The Trial Balance of P Fry on 1 May was as follows:

	Dr £	Cr £
Cash at bank	510	
Debtors	1 100	
Creditors		900
Premises	2 000	
Capital		2 710
	3 610	3 610

Open accounts and enter the balances from the Trial Balance. Enter the following transactions into the books and take out a Trial Balance on 31 May:

		£
May 6	Received by cheques from debtors	750
10	Paid creditors by cheques	800
13	Paid by cheque for extensions to premises	150
20	Sales on credit (including £60 VAT)	460
27	Purchases on credit (including £45 VAT)	345

3 The following information refers to a small wholesale business kept by T Nichols.

Balance Sheet as at 1 May 19—

	£		£
Capital	5 000	Stock	2 300
Creditor		Debtors	
R Mayhew	300	T Wilkins	1 200
		R Watson	800
		Bank balance	1 000
	5 300		5 300

Sales		£
May 8	T Wilkins	850
12	R Watson	1 010
18	T Wilkins	200
		2 060

Sales returns		£
May 20	T Wilkins	48

Purchases		£
May 12	R Mayhew	1 400
21	R Mayhew	500
		1 900

Purchases returns		£
May 14	R Mayhew	180

Cash received and banked		£
May 8	R Wilkins	1 200
9	R Watson	800

Cheques drawn during month		£
May 4	Purchase of office furniture	1 000
17	R Mayhew	300
31	Rent	500
	Drawings	450

You are required to write up T Nichols' ledger for the month of May 19—; a bank account is kept in the ledger, and extract a Trial Balance on 31 May 19—. Ignore VAT. (*RSA BKI*)

4 *a* What is the basic purpose of the Trial Balance?

b If a Trial Balance does not agree what checks would you carry out in order to find the error or errors? (*RSA BKI*)

5 On 31 May 19— the following Trial Balance was extracted from the books of R Wilson:

	£	£
Capital 1 June (in previous year)		50 000
Fixtures and fittings	25 000 +3000	
Delivery vans	20 000	
Trade creditors		3 716
Stock 1 June (in previous year)	8 720	
Trade debtors	5 350	
Cash at bank	4 750	
Cash in hand	376	
Purchases	10 816 +270	
Sales		27 314 -3000
Proprietor's drawings	3 000	
Delivery van expenses	3 018	
	81 030	81 030

A check of the accounts revealed the following errors:

a A customer's account of £50, long overdue should have been written off as a bad debt

b No entry had been made for bank charges £100

c A sale of fixtures and fittings at book value £3 000 had been credited to sales account

d A customer had paid an account in cash £250; the envelope containing the cash had been left in a desk drawer and no entry had been made in the books

e The delivery van expenses includes £500 paid for repairs to R Wilson's private car

f A purchase invoice of £270 had not been entered in the books

Prepare the Trial Balance which would be extracted from R Wilson's books after the corrections have been made. (*RSA BKI*)

6 Mr S Faulkner extracted a Trial Balance at 30 June 19— and because he could not trace the reason for a discrepancy in the totals he placed the difference in a Suspense Account, as follows:

The following errors were discovered later:
a The Purchases Day Book goods column had been overcast by £10.
b A sales invoice of £182.00 entered in the Sales Day Book in June was not posted to Bell & Sons' Account.
c Discount allowed (£36.00) was entered in the Cash Book in June but not posted to Hugh Charles' Account.

You are required to correct these errors in a Journal and post the necessary entries to a Suspense Account.

7 Miss Anne Teeke was made redundant and received £2 000 as redundancy pay. She decided to set up her own business of buying and selling 'period' furniture. She paid £1 000 as capital into a bank account, registered for VAT and rented premises from 1 April. All purchases are strictly on a cash basis, due to the nature of her contacts, with no VAT being chargeable, whilst sales are all on credit plus VAT. The following transactions were carried out in April 19—:

April	2	Withdrew £400 from the bank for business purposes
	2	Cash purchases £250
	4	Paid rent by cheque for April £25
	4	Paid advertising by cheque £20
	9	Sold on credit to Hardcastle Hotel, furniture £300 + VAT £45
	11	Paid rates by cheque (East Town BC) for six months to 30 September 19— £212
	13	Cash purchases £125
	14	Sold to Ullswater Motel, furniture £200 + VAT £30
	14	Drawings from bank £40
	16	Received cheque for £345 from Hardcastle Hotel
	18	Sold to Nutchester Estates, furniture £50 + VAT £7.50
	23	Withdrew £300 from bank for business purposes
	24	Cash purchases £280
	26	Sold to Hardcastle Hotel, furniture £400 + VAT £60
	28	Drawings from bank £40

		Suspense Account				NL38
19—		Details	Fo	Dr £	Cr £	Bal £
June 30		Balance	TB	136.00		136.00

Enter these transactions in the appropriate books, post to the Nominal and Sales Ledgers, balance off the Cash Book and extract a Trial Balance, at 30 April 19—.

Continue by entering the transactions for May which were as follows:

May 2 Received cheque from Hardcastle Hotel for £460

2 Paid rent by cheque for May £25

3 Received cheque from Nutchester Estates for £57.50

9 Withdrew £500 from the bank for business purposes

9 Received cheque returned by bank marked 'R/D insufficient funds' £57.50 (this is the cheque paid into the bank on 3 May)

10 Cash purchases £510

10 After a telephone call to Nutchester Estates, it was agreed to re-present the cheque

14 Drawings from bank £60

16 Sold to Ullswater Motel, furniture £300 + VAT £45

23 Sold to Buckingham Guest House, furniture £350 + VAT £52.50

28 Drawings from bank £60

30 Now prepare the Trial Balance

Continue by entering the transactions for June which were as follows:

June 2 Paid rent by cheque for June £25

6 Received cheque from Ullswater Motel £345

9 Interview with bank manager and obtained an overdraft facility of £1 000

9 Bought second-hand van by cheque £1 205 (including VAT £157)

13 Sold to Hardcastle Hotel, furniture £400 + VAT £57

14 Accepted cheque for £457 from Hardcastle Hotel in full settlement of the sale on 13 June

16 Withdrew £500 from the bank for business purposes

16 Cash purchases of £200 and £250

16 Drawings from bank £60

20 Sold to C Rest Hotel, furniture £320 + VAT £48

24 Sold to M Centrepoint, furniture £40 + VAT £6

28 Paid electricity bill by cheque for lighting and heating £66

28 Paid by cash bill for advertising £17

29 Learned that M Centrepoint had died leaving no net assets: write off the amount owing as a bad debt

30 Drawings from bank £60

30 Extract a Trial Balance at this date

10 Trading Account

10.1 Trading Account

In order to make a profit a business must buy or manufacture goods and sell them at a higher price than they paid for them. In the first year of manufacturing the Faulkner Resteasy Camp Beds they cost £10 each to make and were being sold for £15 each, resulting in a profit of £5 on each one sold. During the whole of the first year 100 of these beds were sold, resulting in a sales figure of:

$$100 \times £15 = £1\,500$$

The cost of sales was: $100 \times £10 = -£1\,000$

Providing a profit of: $£500$

There were 20 left in stock at the end of the first year and these were brought forward as opening stock for the second year when a further 120 were made for the same cost; the selling price was not changed and 110 were sold. The second year's figures show:

Opening stock $(20 \times £10) = £200$ Sales $(110 \times £15)$
Add Manufacturing cost: $= £1\,650$
$120 \times £10)$ $= £1\,200$

Cost of goods offered
for sale $(140 \times £10)$ $= £1\,400$

If the cost of goods offered for sale (£1 400) is deducted from the sales of £1 650, it would appear that a profit of only £250 had been made. This is not, however, the true profit figure, because if 110 were sold at a profit of £5 each, then the profit would be £550 (ie $110 \times £5$). The difference between the £550 and £250 figures is £300 and this is explained by the value of the stock at the end of the second year (closing stock). As 140 were available for sale and only 110 were sold there should be 30 (ie $140 - 110$) in stock at the end realising a stock figure of £300 (ie $30 \times £10$). The stock figures at the beginning and at the end of a trading period are, therefore, essential in calculating profit.

In trading account form these calculations appear as follows:

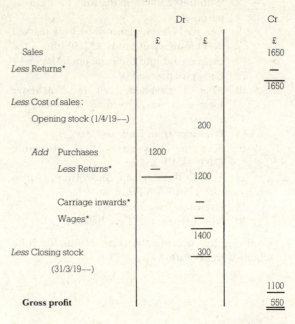

Trading Account of P Faulkner & Sons
for the year ended 31 March 19—

	Dr		Cr
	£	£	£
Sales			1650
Less Returns*			—
			1650
Less Cost of sales:			
Opening stock (1/4/19—)		200	
Add Purchases	1200		
Less Returns*	—	1200	
Carriage inwards*		—	
Wages*		—	
		1400	
Less Closing stock		300	
(31/3/19—)			
			1100
Gross profit			550

* These items, although not required for this example, are inserted to indicate how they would be treated if they were included in a more detailed trading account.

It will be seen that the Trading Account is used as a means of calculating gross profit. Gross profit is the excess of the selling price over the cost price plus any direct expenses in acquiring the goods such as carriage inwards and wages.

When the figures for sales, purchases and cost of sales are used in calculating percentage margins and rates of turnover they should be net, ie sales should have sales returns deducted; purchases should have purchases returns deducted; cost of sales should have added to it any costs which affect the cost before being offered for sale. These include carriage inwards, ie transport costs in bringing goods into the business (but not carriage outwards), wages paid in making or improving the goods such as bottling, blending, etc.

10.2 Percentage margins

This simply means the percentage of profit and it can be expressed in two ways:

1 On cost – when it is called **mark-up**
2 On the selling price (sales) – when it is called **margin**

The percentage margins involved in selling the Faulkner Resteasy camp beds are:

$$\text{Mark-up} = \frac{\text{Gross profit} \times 100}{\text{Cost of sales}} = \frac{\overset{1}{\cancel{550}} \times 100}{\underset{2}{\cancel{1100}}} = 50\%$$

$$\text{Margin} = \frac{\text{Gross profit} \times 100}{\text{Sales}} = \frac{\overset{1}{\cancel{550}} \times 100}{\underset{3}{\cancel{1650}}} = 33\tfrac{1}{3}\%$$

The same answers will be obtained if the cost per unit (ie each camp bed) is used:

$$\text{Mark-up} = \frac{\text{Gross profit} \times 100}{\text{Cost of sale}} = \frac{\overset{1}{\cancel{5}} \times 100}{\underset{2}{\cancel{10}}} = 50\%$$

$$\text{Margin} = \frac{\text{Gross profit} \times 100}{\text{Selling price}} = \frac{\overset{1}{\cancel{5}} \times 100}{\underset{3}{\cancel{15}}} = 33\tfrac{1}{3}\%$$

10.3 Rate of turnover

Turnover is another term for sales and the rate of turnover indicates how quickly stock is being moved (or sold). A business becomes more efficient when it speeds up its rate of turnover, ie the number of times the average amount of stock is sold in a year.

To calculate rate of turnover use this formula:

$$\frac{\text{Cost of sales}}{\text{Average stock}}$$

Note: Average stock $= \dfrac{\text{Opening stock} + \text{Closing stock}}{2}$

Faulkners rate of turnover for the second year for Resteasy camp beds was:

$$\frac{1100}{(200 + 300) \div 2} = \frac{1100}{250} = \underline{\underline{4.4}}$$

Exercises

1 At 1 January 19—, Brian Jenkins had 1 500 articles in stock which had cost him £2 each. During the month of January, he purchased 2 000 more articles at the same price. He sold 2 500 at £3.00 each and 100 at £2.50 each.

   a Draw up a simple stock record to show the number of items in stock at the end of the month.

   b Prepare his Trading Account for the month of January to show clearly the cost of sales and gross profit. (*RSA BKI*)

2 From the following figures which relate to the financial year ended 31 December 19— prepare the Trading Account of James Brown. The account should show clearly net purchases, cost of goods offered for sale, cost of sales and net sales:

	£
Purchases	18 500
Sales	30 350
Stock (1 January 19—)	2 100
Sales returns	350
Purchases returns	500
Carriage inwards	40
Wages	2 500
Stock (31 December 19—)	640

3 Calculate for Faulkner Resteasy camp beds for this year:

   a the percentage margin and

   b the rate of turnover from the following information (calculations to be correct to one decimal place):

Sales:	150 @ £15.75 (as per price list)
Opening stock:	30 @ £10.00
Production (purchases):	146 @ £10.50
Closing stock:	26 @ £10.50

4 Calculate the percentage margins and mark-up from Faulkner's price list on p 39 for each commodity given the following cost prices:

Cat No	Cost £	Cat No	Cost £
734T	170.00	14SB	13.00
754T	140.00	15SB	12.00
774T	110.00	27R	18.00
523T	108.00	29R	13.00
553T	84.00	31R	10.75
583T	70.00	81C	10.50
13SB	13.50		

11 Profit and Loss Account

Unit 10 dealt with the calculation of gross profit in the Trading Account and it was seen that the profit from sales was arrived at after allowing for the direct costs of buying or making the goods. In addition to these direct costs a business has to pay overhead costs (referred to in Unit 1) such as administration expenses covering rent, rates, lighting, heating, insurance, salaries of office staff, health and safety provisions, as well as distribution costs such as carriage outwards to customers, advertising, salaries of sales personnel, etc. When the overheads are deducted from gross profit the business expects to make a net profit, but if the overheads exceed the gross profit there will be a net trading loss. The expenses relating to the period during which the profit is calculated have to be 'written off' or transferred to the profit and loss account: the expenses to the Dr column and the income to the Cr column. This is done by means of Journal entries, as in Fig 45.

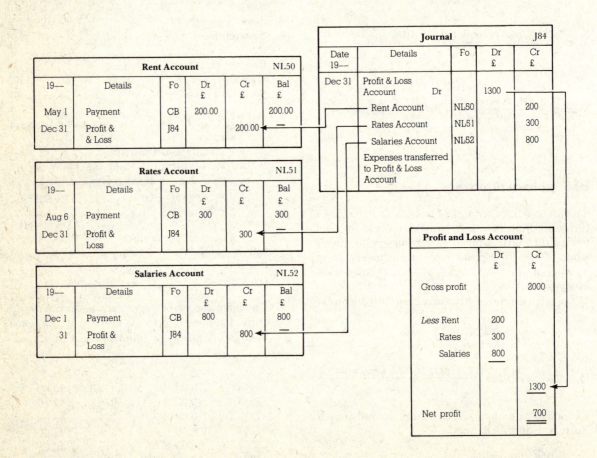

Fig 45   Nominal ledger containing overhead expense accounts

11.1 Accruals, prepayments and depreciation

More often than not the amounts in the Nominal Ledger Expense Accounts do not correspond with the period covered by the accounts when calculating profit. In this connection there will usually be:

Accruals   Amounts still to be paid for – variously described as due, owing, in arrears, outstanding or accrued. The accrual is *added* to the amount actually paid in order to arrive at the actual expense, which is the sum transferred to the Profit and Loss Account.

Example: in Faulkner's Trial Balance on p 104 the electricity was paid on 6 April but according to the meter reading taken on 30 April there was a further £12.73 owing (an accrual).

Prepayments   Any item already paid for but not yet received – variously described as paid in advance, unexpired or prepaid.

The prepayment is *deducted* from the amount actually paid to arrive at the amount used, which is the sum transferred to the Profit and Loss Account.

Example: in Faulkner's Trial Balance on p 104 rent was paid for April, May and June. The amounts for May and June were, therefore, paid in advance, resulting in a prepayment of £200 on 30 April.

Similarly, the rates of £520 were for the whole year 1 April to 31 March next year, consequently 11 months of rates (£477) were paid in advance on 30 April.

Depreciation   This is the loss in value of an asset over a period of time, the most usual cause being wear and tear especially for motor vehicles. An estimate of the loss in value (an expense) has to be made and charged (debited) to the Profit and Loss Account.

Example: Faulkners estimated 10% depreciation per annum on the machinery and equipment. 10% of £420 ÷ 12 (for one month) = £3.50

The ledger accounts for rent, rates, and lighting and heating are now illustrated below, together with the 'adjustments' for accruals and prepayments and the journalised transfers to the Profit and Loss Account of P Faulkner & Sons for the month of April. Notes follow, on p 114.

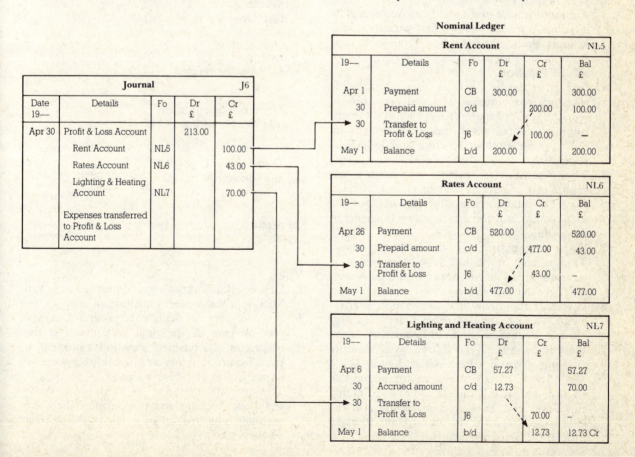

Notes: Rent Account ⎫ These accounts are credited to
Rates Account ⎭ take the values out of April and debited to put the same values into May (assets)

Lighting and Heating Account — This account was debited to put the value already received into April, but not yet paid, and credited in May to show the amount owing (liability)

The Profit and Loss Account is debited with the full expense.

Guidelines for the preparation of the Profit and Loss Account (combined with the Trading Account):

1 As the Profit and Loss Account is an account it should be correctly titled and comply with the principles of double entry. The bracketed headings are shown in the account opposite for guidance only and can be dispensed with when competence is gained.
2 It is normal practice to combine the Trading Account with the Profit and Loss Account. The Trading Account is shown first with its result, ie gross profit of £160; if a Profit and Loss Account only has to be prepared the gross profit will be supplied.
3 Any other income such as discount received, rent received, interest received, commission received is added to the gross profit in the credit column to obtain total income; if there is no other income omit total income and deduct the expenses.
4 The expenses (ie revenue expenditure not capital expenditure or drawings) are deducted from the total income after allowing for the prepayments and accruals to obtain the figure of net profit.
5 When working from a Trial Balance to prepare Trading and Profit and Loss Accounts it is recommended that the working column is used to clarify the calculations.
6 Details of the value of closing stock, prepayments, accruals and depreciation are often supplied at the foot of the Trial Balance as notes.
7 Work through the Trial Balance systematically grouping items together such as debtors (£184 + £115 + £30 = £329) and creditors, and tick off each item as it is transferred to the Trading and Profit and Loss Account. Tick also the information used for the adjustments to make sure all the items are dealt with.

8 The unticked items plus the adjustments (cross-ticked when preparing the balance sheet) are now either assets or liabilities which are shown in the Balance Sheet (Unit 12).

Trading and Profit & Loss Account of P Faulkner
for the month ended 30 April 19—

	(Working column) £	(Debit) £	(Credit) £
Sales			260.00
Less **Cost of sales:**			
Opening stock		1 200.00	
Add Purchases		200.00	
		1 400.00	
Less Closing stock		1 300.00	
			100.00
Gross profit			160.00
Add Commission received			87.00
Total Income			247.00
Less **Expenses:**			
Rent paid	300.00		
Less Amount prepaid	200.00		
		100.00	
Rates paid	520.00		
Less Amount prepaid	477.00		
		43.00	
Lighting and heating paid	57.27		
Add Amount owing	12.73		
		70.00	
Depreciation of machinery and equipment		3.00	
			216.00
Net profit			31.00

Notes
1 Depreciation was not allowed for the motor van because it was a recent acquisition.
2 It is necessary to calculate the profit or loss each year as part of the final accounts, but the proprietor of a business may find it prudent to know his profit or loss on a monthly basis and so be warned of any danger signals.
3 The amounts entered in the Trading and Profit and Loss Account and the Balance Sheet are normally rounded up or down to the nearest whole pound.

11.2 Capital and revenue expenditure

All items of expenditure are debited to their appropriate ledger accounts but they are quite different from the expenditure involved in purchasing goods for resale. When Faulkners bought a new delivery van, a typewriter and paid for an extension to their offices this was **capital** expenditure because they were purchased with the intention of keeping them for a long time; they resulted in the firm acquiring additional assets and increasing their earning capacity. This expenditure does not affect either the profit or the capital. In other words, Faulkners are neither better off nor worse off in monetary terms as a result of these purchases.

Revenue expenditure (or 'overheads'), on the other hand, relates to the day-to-day running expenses of the business, such as rates, electricity, salaries and motor expenses. As these expenses are deducted from the firm's income they reduce both the profit and the capital and they are entered in the Trading and Profit and Loss Account.

Example: The purchase of a building for a new store (an asset) is capital expenditure but the cost of advertising to announce when it will be opened (an expense deducted from profit) is revenue expenditure.

The treatment of these two categories of expenditure and their effect on the business are very different and it is crucial that all involved with the recording of accounts are able to distinguish revenue expenditure from capital expenditure.

Exercises

1 The following Trial Balance was extracted from the books of David Jones at the close of business on 31 December 19—:

	£	£
Capital Account 1 January 19—		4 104
Drawings	3 000	
Fixtures and fittings	800	
Insurance	405	
Rent and rates	1 240	
Wages and salaries	1 900	
Discounts allowed and received	440	210
Bad debts	304	
Trade debtors	1 251	
Trade creditors		1 254
Stock – 1 January 19—	1 508	
Purchases	9 040	
Sales		16 170
Cash in hand	210	
Cash at bank	1 090	
Purchase returns		320
Sales returns	505	
Postage and stationery	260	
Carriage outwards	105	
	22 058	22 058

From this Trial Balance, and from the notes given below, you are required to prepare the Trading and Profit and Loss Account of David Jones for the year ended 31 December 19—.
Note: A Balance Sheet is *not* required.

a Stock 31 December 19— £1 610
b Wages and salaries accrued, due at 31 December 19— £65
c Rates are prepaid on 31 December 19— £115
d A further £60 bad debts are to be written off
e There is a stock of stamps to the value of £14 at 31 December 19—   (*RSA BKI*)

2 The following Trial Balance was extracted from the books of C Lord on 30 April 19—. You are required to prepare his Trading and Profit and Loss Accounts for the year ended 30 April 19—.

The Trading Account should show the cost of goods sold.

Trial Balance at 30 April 19—

	Dr £	Cr £
Loan from W Paris		5 000
Capital		16 850
Drawings	4 600	
Telephone	200	
Wages	2 650	
Bank and Cash	8 800	
Salaries	6 000	
Purchases and sales	22 000	44 000
Debtors and creditors	6 000	8 000
Motor expenses	2 350	
Office expenses	2 500	
Light and heat	1 700	
Rates	600	
Premises	10 000	
Fixtures and fittings	1 800	
Vehicles	2 000	
Stock at 1 May 19—	2 000	
Carriage inwards	450	
Sales and purchase returns	300	150
Discounts allowed and received	250	200
	74 200	74 200

The following additional information as at 30 April 19— is also available:

a Stock on 30 April 19— was £3 500
b Wages owing but not yet paid £50
c Rates paid in advance are £100
d Light, heat and rates for the year are apportioned
   ¼ to Trading Account
   ¾ to Profit and Loss Account
e Interest at 10% per annum is to be paid on the loan

Note: A Balance Sheet is not required.

(*RSA BKI*)

3 *a* Explain the meaning of the following accounting terms:

   Capital expenditure
   Revenue (income)
   Revenue expenditure

b J Donald is an estate agent and below are some of his transactions. Rule up three columns headed: Capital expenditure, Revenue expenditure, Revenue (income), and list the items in the appropriate columns.

Commission received   Purchase of photo-
Office rent   copying machine
Fees charged to   Commission paid
clients for   Cost of installing win-
professional services   dow display fitment

(*RSA BKI*)

4 Hawkins & Sons deal in typewriters and accessories. State whether the following items are capital or revenue expenditure, giving reasons for your answers:

a *i* The purchase of 14 typewriters as stock in trade.
   ii The purchase of 4 new tyres for the firm's delivery van.
   iii The payment of an insurance premium on the firm's premises.
   iv The payment of an annual Christmas bonus to the staff.
   v The purchase of 2 new electric typewriters for office use.

b The firm's Profit and Loss Account includes an item of £2100 for repairs, redecoration and alterations to their freehold premises. If it is decided to charge two thirds of this sum as capital expenditure, what effect would this have on the firm's Balance Sheet?

(*RSA BKI*)

12 Balance Sheet and Capital and Drawings Accounts

A Balance Sheet is not an account and therefore does not contain transfers from any of the ledger accounts. It is generally defined as: *a statement of how a business stands at a certain point in time.* It is a summary of all ledger balances after calculating profit.

The Balance Sheet illustrated (p 118) and recommended is in a vertical format; the practice of displaying the assets and liabilities in a two-sided format is seldom used today.

12.1 Marshalling the assets

This is the process of arranging the assets in order and in groups.

Assets

The possessions of a firm or person are divided into two categories (fixed and current) and the totals of each group are shown in the Balance Sheet.

Fixed assets   The possessions which are acquired with the intention of keeping them for a considerable time; they are acquired by capital expenditure and include such items as buildings, machinery, motor vehicles, computers, office furniture, etc.

Current assets   These include items in current use, such as stock-in-trade, debtors and money.

Liabilities

The debts owing by a firm or person (excluding the capital – see below) and they can also be divided into two groups and the totals of each group are shown in the Balance Sheet.

Long term   These include liabilities which do not have to be met in the immediate future such as mortgages and long-term loans.

Current   The debts which have to be met in the near future such as creditors, VAT and short-term loans.

Capital

Capital is the amount invested in the business by the proprietor(s) and it is the difference between the total assets and total liabilities. It represents the value of the firm's net assets owing to the owner(s).

Procedure for drawing up a Balance Sheet

1   The title should contain: the title of the document (Balance Sheet); the business name; the date on which the balances were extracted.
2   List the fixed assets first with the net values in the right-hand column; where depreciation is involved this should be shown as illustrated on p 118 by using the analysis columns and deducting it from the previous value. Total the net 'book' values of the fixed assets.
3   List the current assets in the order indicated and total them.
4   List the current liabilities in the order indicated and total them under current assets.
5   Deduct the current liabilities from the current assets to arrive at the working capital which should be entered in the right-hand column. Working capital is the amount of net current assets available for the immediate needs of the business.
6   Add working capital to the fixed assets to arrive at total net assets.
7   In order to check the Balance Sheet and show how the business is financed under 'Represented by' enter the previous capital; add the net profit; deduct the drawings and the amount remaining is the new amount of capital on the date of the Balance Sheet. (*Note:* Drawings do not affect the business trading figures and they should not be entered in the Profit and Loss Account; they can be in the form of goods or cash.)
8   List the long-term liabilities and add the total to the new capital figure.

12.2 Capital and Drawings Accounts

The Capital Account has a credit balance as it is a liability of the firm to the owner(s). Any profit made by the firm increases the capital and likewise any loss made by the firm reduces the capital. This is reflected in the completion of the double entry cycle when the net profit from the Profit and Loss Account is transferred to the credit column of the Capital Account by a Journal entry.

For convenience a record of drawings is kept in a Drawings Account until such time as a Balance Sheet is prepared. The Drawings Account is debited each time the owner draws out cash or goods for his own use; the total of all the drawings is transferred by a debit entry in the Capital Account (through the Journal) and this amount appears in the Balance Sheet as a deduction from capital.

The following accounts illustrate the effect of drawings and profit on the capital invested by the proprietor:

Capital Account   Nl.3

19–	Details	Fo	Dr £	Cr £	Bal £
Apr 1	Balance	J1		2000.00	2000.00
30	Net profit	J10		31.00	2031.00
30	Drawings	J10	60.00		1971.00 Cr

Drawings Account   Nl.9

19––	Details	Fo	Dr £	Cr £	Bal £
Apr 29	Payment (Holiday deposit)	J10	60.00		60.00'
30	Transfer to Capital Account	J10		60.00	—

Balance Sheet of P Faulkner
as at 30 April 19—

	Cost £	Depre- ciation £	Book value £
Fixed assets			
Machinery and equipment	420.00	3.00	417.00
Motor van	1 200.00	—	1 200.00
	1 620.00	3.00	1 617.00

Current assets		
Stock		1 300.00
Debtors		329.00
Prepaid rent		200.00
Prepaid rates		477.00
Cash in hand		10.00
		2 316.00

Current liabilities		
Creditors	1 630.00	
VAT	9.00	
Bank overdraft	310.00	
Electricity owing	13.00	
	1 962.00	

Working capital
(£2 316 − £1 962)   354.00

Total net assets   1 971.00

Represented by:
Capital (1 April 19—)   2 000.00
Add Net profit   31.00

    2 031.00
Less Drawings   60.00

    1 971.00

Long term liabilities (added to final capital)   —

Exercises

1 George Smith is in the process of preparing his accounts for the year ended 30 April 19—. His net profit for the year was calculated as £12 000 and during the year he has withdrawn £7 000 for his own use. On 30 April 19— he decides to withdraw a further £1 000 and to leave the remainder in the business. After completing his Profit and Loss Account the following balances remain on Smith's books.

	£
Capital at 1 May 19—	21 000
Freehold property	20 000
Motor vehicles	8 000
Long-term loan	6 000
Stock	2 000
Balance at bank	685
Debtors	2 400
Creditors	2 000

You are informed that:
a wages of £100 were outstanding
b insurance has been prepaid by £15
c closing stock has been undervalued by £1 000
Prepare:
  i George Smith's Capital Account showing the entries for the year up to 30 April 19—
  ii George Smith's Balance Sheet on 30 April 19— showing clearly therein the values of his fixed assets, current assets, current liabilities, long-term liabilities and capital on this date. (*RSA BKI*)

2 Owen Williams prepared the following Trial Balance at 31 December 19— after drafting his Trading Account:

	£	£
Trade debtors	9 300	
Trade creditors		11 650
Bank		4 500
Capital		48 300
Rent and rates	2 600	
Drawings	9 000	
Freehold premises	30 600	
Heat and light	1 650	
Wages and salaries	7 550	
Cash in hand	1 700	
Motor vehicle expenses	2 500	
Carriage outwards	800	
Motor vehicles	5 200	
Advertising	2 000	
Gross profit		21 000
Stock 31 December 19—	12 550	
	£85 450	£85 450

You are given the following information:
a Provide for carriage outwards owing £200
b An electricity bill for £300 for the quarter ended 31 December 19— had not been paid
c The advertising expenditure shown above includes £1 600 for a television contract due to commence on 1 January 19—
You are required to prepare the Profit and Loss Account for the year ended 31 December 19— and a Balance Sheet as at 31 December 19—. (*RSA BKI*)

3 George Price is the proprietor of a small business. He keeps his financial records on double entry principles and extracted the following Trial Balance on 31 May 19—:

	£		£
Stock 1 June 19—	7 000	Capital 1 June 19—	85 000
Cash at bank	8 000	Creditors	3 700
Furniture and fittings	7 500	Sales	40 000
Premises	65 000		
Rates	1 600		
Purchases	30 000		
Heating and lighting	1 500		
Cleaning	1 700		
Packing materials	1 400		
Drawings	5 000		
	128 700		128 700

You are required to take the following into consideration on 31 May 19—:

		£
a	Stock on hand	9 500
b	Rates paid in advance	400
c	Stock of packing material	300

and prepare a Trading and Profit and Loss Account for the year ended 31 May 19— and a Balance Sheet at that date. (*RSA BKI*)

4 The following balances remain in William Dean's books after completion of the Trading and Profit and Loss Accounts for the year ended 31 May 19—:

	£	£
Capital 1 June 19—		124 000
Net profit for the year ended 31 May 19—		13 800
Loan from John Dean (repayable in 10 years time)		9 500
Trade creditors		1 950
Expense creditors		270
Premises	110 000	
Stock in trade	25 000	
Trade debtors	2 600	
Balance at bank	1 400	
Cash in hand	20	
Expense items paid in advance	500	
Proprietor's drawings	10 000	
	149 520	149 520

You are required to:
a Set out William Dean's Balance Sheet as at 31 May 19—. Your Balance Sheet should show long-term and current liabilities: fixed and current assets.
b Write up William Dean's Capital Account as it would appear in his private ledger for the year ended 31 May 19—. (*RSA BKI*)

5 Prepare the Trading and Profit and Loss Accounts for Anne Teeke's first three months of trading and a Balance Sheet as at 30 June 19— from the figures supplied in Exercise 7 of Unit 9 (p 108).

You are required to take the following into consideration: closing stock at 30 June 19—, £200; motor expenses owing, £34. Rates are prepaid for three months.

6 You have now been put in charge of the ledger accounts at P Faulkner & Sons. The list of ledger balances at 28 February 19— is given in the Trial Balance below and details on p 121. You are required to carry out the following tasks:

Task No 1: Transfer the ledger balances as at 1 March into three separate ledgers, namely Sales Ledger, Purchases Ledger and Nominal Ledger (for accounts other than debtors and creditors). Enter the cash and bank balances on the same date in a Cash Book.

Task No 2: Enter the transactions for March (listed on p 121) in the appropriate books, post to the ledgers, and extract a trial balance at 31 March. (If your Trial Balance does not agree enter the difference into a Suspense Account to cause the Trial Balance to agree) and proceed to:

Task No 3: Prepare the final accounts for the quarter ending 31 March after taking into account:
a Stock at 31 March 19— was valued at £8 500
b Prepayments: rates £857 and advertising £250
c Accrued lighting and heating £1 107

P Faulkner & Sons
Trial Balance at 28 February 19—

Accounts	Dr £	Cr £
Capital		100 000
Buildings	62 000	
Machinery and equipment	25 000	
Stock at 1 January 19—	10 000	
Delivery vans	4 400	
Wages and salaries	27 000	
Purchases	46 500	
Purchases returns		500
Sales		110 700
Sales returns	700	
Debtors } see separate	10 000	
Creditors } list on p 121		4 000
VAT		800
Advertising	5 500	
Rates	2 000	
Office expenses	13 000	
Lighting and heating	1 500	
Cash at bank	8 388	
Cash in hand	12	
	216 000	216 000

Debtors at 28 February 19—	£	Creditors at 28 February 19—	£
J G Andrews	2 300	NKG plc	1 000
Bailey Brothers	3 000	Tape Works Ltd	536
Carters Sports	4 000	CIC plc	734
Edna Davies	700	Fettlenold & Sons	1 730
	10 000		4 000

Transactions for March 19—
(All purchases and sales are on credit; all receipts and payments are by cheque, except where otherwise shown.)

		Goods £	+VAT £
March 1	Sold to J G Andrews	2 600	390
2	Purchases from NKG plc	740	111
3	Paid Southampton BC for rates £917		
4	Received from J G Andrews £2 300		
5	Received from Bailey Bros £2 536		
8	Sold to Bailey Bros	3 100	465
10	Withdrew cash from bank £50		
11	Purchases from Tape Works Ltd	340	51
15	Paid NKG plc £734		
15	Paid Tape Works Ltd £536		
15	Paid Fettlenold & Sons £1 730		
16	Paid in cash for advertisement in EW News £50		
17	Sold to Carters Sports	4 300	645
18	Paid lighting and heating £533		
19	Paid for advertisement in *Guardian* £500		
22	Purchases from CIC plc	920	138
23	Received from Carters Sports £7 164		
30	Paid wages £3 000		

13 **Wages**

In many industries, wages form the biggest element in the cost of production, therefore it is essential to keep accurate records and control over the payment of these.

At Faulkners the cost of the materials used in production and the cost of wages were of equal value.

There is no difference in the method of recording salaries but it is customary to pay them monthly by cheque or credit transfer, whereas wages are normally paid weekly in cash.

At Faulkners this is done by means of a clock card which each worker inserts in a time recording (or clocking-in) machine at the time of entering and leaving the works. An example of a clock card is shown below (Fig 46).

For costing and checking purposes a record must be kept of the time spent by each employee on each job; this is done on a daily time sheet. Each week the clock cards are passed to the Wages Section, who also obtain the daily time sheets and check that each worker's time and job hours agree before making out the wages.

13.1 Time and job cards

In order to calculate the wages a record must be kept of the time spent by each worker at his work.

CLOCK CARD

No 381   Name: T RAWLINGS

Week ending: 13 May 19—

Day	In	Out	In	Out	TOTAL HOURS
M	0800	1201	1302	1739	8.75
Tu	0758	1200	1300	1730	8.50
W	0802	1202	1301	1800	9.00
Th	0810	1200	1301	1731	8.25
F	0801	1203	1258	1601	7.00
TOTAL					41.50

	£
Ordinary time: . . . 38 hrs @ £2.00 (up to 38 hours)	76.00
Overtime . . . . . . 3.5 hrs @ £3.00	10.50
TOTAL GROSS WAGES	86.50

Fig 46 Clock card

Once the hours are agreed the wages are calculated and then entered in the wages records.

The clock card illustrated in Fig 46 relates to Mr T Rawlings for the week ended 13 May 19—. This card, along with all the cards for all employees, is collected from the clocking-in machine racks at the end of the week and handed in to the Wages Office.

A calculator can be used for multiplying the number of hours by the rate per hour. Each day's total is calculated to the nearest quarter of an hour.

In this example, Mr Rawlings spent 8 hours 38 minutes at work on Monday and he is credited with $8\frac{3}{4}$ hours (8.75) as the 8 minutes in excess of 30 is nearer to the next quarter which allows him to claim 15 minutes. This employee is paid at the rate of £2 per hour for a 38 hour week and time and a half thereafter, which is regarded as overtime. These amounts are calculated on the clock cards in the Wages Office and, in the case of Mr Rawlings, he has worked a total of $41\frac{1}{2}$ hours of which 38 are paid at the rate of £2 per hour (£76.00) and $3\frac{1}{2}$ hours at £3 per hour (£10.50) giving him a total gross wage for the week of £86.50.

The clock cards provide the information to be entered in the wages records, including the pay slip which the employees receive with their pay.

Exercises

1   Calculate the gross pay for each of the following employees whose basic rate of pay is £2.40 per hour for a 36 hour week; time and a quarter for the next 6 hours and time and a half thereafter:

   J Adams   38 hours   J Smith   44 hours
   T Spinks   34 hours   R Williams   40 hours

2   The employee whose clock card no 38 is shown below is paid at £2.80 per hour for a 42 hour week; time and a quarter for the next 6 hours and time and a half thereafter. Calculate his gross weekly wage.

3   a   Calculate the daily and weekly total hours worked, the amount of pay for ordinary time and the amount of pay for overtime for the employee whose clock card no 123 is given below. The current rate of pay is £1.80 per hour for a 38 hour week and time and a half thereafter, which is regarded as overtime.

   b   From 1 November a new pay scale was negotiated increasing the basic pay to £2.00 per hour for a 36 hour week. What difference will this make to Mr Browning's gross pay if he works the same number of hours as above?

No 38					
Name W Scott					
Week Ending 4 June 19—					
Day	In	Out	In	Out	Total
AM M PM	0800	1201	1300	1800	
AM Tu PM	0759	1230	1330	1730	
AM W PM	0802	1202	1300	1900	
AM Th PM	0758	1201	1300	1800	
AM F PM	0800	1230	1330	1900	
AM S PM	0830	1230	1300	1700	
AM Su PM					
Ordinary time					
Overtime					
Total wages					
Less Nat Ins					
Income tax					
	Amount paid				

CLOCK CARD					
No 123				Name: J R BROWNING	
Week ending: 8 October 19—					
Day	In	Out	In	Out	TOTAL HOURS
M	0730	1201	1302	1700	
Tu	0728	1158	1300	1701	
W	0731	1202	1301	1659	
Th	0740	1201	1304	1712	
F	0730	1202	1303	1604	
TOTAL					
Ordinary time: . . . . . hrs @ (up to 38 hours)					£
Overtime . . . . hrs @					
TOTAL GROSS WAGES					

13.2 Deductions from pay

Income tax and national insurance are statutory deductions, ie required by law. There are, however, other deductions which are voluntary, such as subscriptions to the social club, savings, benevolent fund etc.

Savings and social club contributions are *fixed* deductions which do not normally change from one week to the next, but income tax and national insurance are *variable* deductions which are linked to the gross pay and may vary from week to week. The variable amounts are calculated each week or month and recorded on a deductions working sheet (form P11, see p 125) or an alternative pay form in the following manner:

1 Enter the gross pay from the clock card, as described in Section 13.1, in column 2.
2 Add (1) to the total of all previous payments made to the employee since 6 April (the first day of the income-tax year) and enter the new total in column 3.
3 Calculate the amount of 'free pay' to which the employee is entitled, in accordance with his code number (which represents the allowances to which he is entitled) and enter this in column 4. This is calculated by looking up the code number in Table A (free pay table) in the tax tables.
4 Subtract the 'free pay' in (3) from the total gross pay to date in (2) to arrive at the amount of 'taxable pay', which is then entered in column 5.
5 Calculate the total tax due to date by reference to the amount of 'taxable pay' in Tables B to D (taxable pay tables) and enter this sum in column 6.
6 Subtract the amount of tax already deducted from the total tax due to date in (5) to arrive at the amount to be deducted from the employee's gross pay on the pay day in question and enter it in column 7. Sometimes, for example if the employee has worked a short week, the figure of total tax shown by the tax tables may be less than the tax already deducted; in that case the wages clerk must refund the difference to the employee instead of making any deduction and must enter this amount in column 7 with the initial 'R'.
7 The amount of the national insurance contribution is calculated on the basis of gross pay received by reference to the National Insurance contribution tables or on a percentage basis, and the total of the employee's and employer's

contributions are entered in column 1a and the employee's contribution in column 1b.

The deductions working sheet (Fig 47) relates to Mr T Rawlings (see Fig 46). In the week when his code number was increased from 210 to 260 he was entitled to a refund of income tax. The code number and any amendments made to it during the year are recorded at the top of the deductions working sheet.

8 If an employee has been absent because of illness and he has received statutory sick pay these amounts are recorded in column 1d.

Exercises

1 Calculate an employee's income tax and national insurance contributions for weeks 1–12 and record the entries on a deductions working sheet. His code number was 130L.

Week no	Gross pay in the week	Amended code
	£	
1	70	
2	70	
3	70	
4	70	
5	75	
6	75	
7	25	
8	25	
9	80	
10	80	150L
11	80	
12	78	

2 Calculate an employee's income tax for weeks 24–30 and write the entries on his deductions working sheet. Up to and including week 23 he had received £2 200.00 gross pay; £351.90 had been paid in tax. His code number was 230H.

Week no	Gross pay (£) in the week	Amended code
24	90	
25	90	
26	94	
27	94	
28	94	260H
29	94	
30	46	

Deductions working sheet P11 (New)

Employer's name: P FAULKNER & SONS
Tax District and reference: _____

Employee's surname (in BLOCK letters): RAWLINGS
First two forenames: THOMAS

National Insurance no.	Works no etc.	Date of birth in figures (Day/Month/Year)	Date of leaving in figures (Day/Month/Year)	Tax Code†	Amended code†	Week/Month no. in which applied	Year to 5 April 19......
ST 36 21 38 B	21			210H	260H	4	

National Insurance Contributions*

1a Total of Employee's and Employer's Contributions payable £	1b Employee's contributions payable £	1c Employee's contrib-utions at Contracted-out rate included in Col. 1b £	1d Statutory sick pay in the week or month included in col 2 £
15 59	6 86		
15 59	6 86		
16 20	7 13		
15 59	6 86		
17 74	7 81		

PAYE Income Tax

WEEK number	MONTH number	2 Pay in the week or month including statutory sick pay £	3 Total pay to date £	4 Total free pay to date as shown by Table A £	5 Total taxable pay to date £	6 Total tax due to date as shown by Taxable Pay Tables £	7 Tax deducted or refunded in the week or month Mark refunds "R" £	For employer's use
1	6 April to 5 May — 1	76 00	76 00	40 56	35 44	10 50	10 50	
2		76 00	152 00	81 12	70 88	21 00	10 50	
3		79 00	231 00	121 68	109 32	32 70	11 70	
4	6 May to 5 June — 2	76 00	307 00	200 72	106 28	31 80	0 90	R
5		86 50	393 50	250 90	142 60	42 60	10 80	
6								
7								
8	6 June to 5 July — 3							
9								
10								
11								
12	6 July to 5 Aug — 4							
13								
14								
15								
16								
17	6 Aug to 5 Sept — 5							
18								
19								
20								
21	6 Sept to 5 Oct — 6							
22								
23								
24								
25								
26	6 Oct to 5 Nov — 7							
27								
28								
29								
30								

Total carried forward	Total carried forward	Total carried forward	Total carried forward	Total carried forward

A ▼

*N.I. Contribution Table letter must be entered overleaf beside the N.I. totals boxes – see the note shown there.

This box may be used if the employer wishes to record the N.I. letter while this side of the sheet is in use

† If amended cross out previous code

∅ If in any week/month the amount in column 4 is more than the amount in column 3, make no entry in column 5.

P11 (New)

SPECIMEN

Fig 47 Deductions working sheet

3 You are required to complete the entries on tax deduction cards for week no 5 for the employees listed below:

Name	Code no	Gross wages up to week no 4	Tax paid up to week no 4.	Gross wages in week no 5
		£	£	£
J Perkins	159L	240	35.10	60
S Smith { weeks 1–4	159L	280	47.10	70
{ week 5	220H			
G Thompson	200H	400	73.50	105 (increased from £100 this week)

(RSA OPII)

4 With reference to J Clarke's deductions working sheet on p 127:

a Complete the entry for week no 6 on a deductions working sheet.

b What circumstances could lead to this employee receiving the refund of tax in week no 5?

c Explain how the wages clerk would know *i* the amount of free pay, and *ii* the total tax due in each week.

d Explain how the wages clerk would know the amount of employee's national insurance contributions entered in column no 1.

(RSA OPII – amended)

13.3 Recording wages

The gross pay calculated from the clock cards, or a standard wage if the employee is paid at an agreed amount, together with the deductions, is recorded in the following documents:

1 Wages sheet (or book) normally referred to as the payroll.

2 Employee's pay record sheet which may replace the deductions working sheet.

3 Pay slip for the employee, to advise him of the amount of pay and deductions for the week or other period.

The principal stages in the procedure for paying wages in cash are illustrated opposite.

Note: References are made to the payroll illustrated in Fig 48 on p 128.

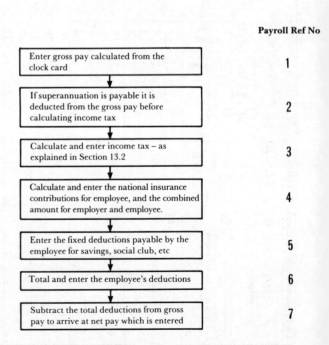

Payroll Ref No

Enter gross pay calculated from the clock card	1
If superannuation is payable it is deducted from the gross pay before calculating income tax	2
Calculate and enter income tax – as explained in Section 13.2	3
Calculate and enter the national insurance contributions for employee, and the combined amount for employer and employee.	4
Enter the fixed deductions payable by the employee for savings, social club, etc	5
Total and enter the employee's deductions	6
Subtract the total deductions from gross pay to arrive at net pay which is entered	7

Deductions working sheet P11 (New)

Employer's name	P FAULKNER & SONS
Employee's surname (in BLOCK letters)	CLARKE
First two forenames	JOAN
Tax District and reference	
National Insurance no.	PR 43 25 35 S
Date of birth in figures (Day | Month | Year)	
Works no. etc.	18
Date of leaving in figures (Day | Month | Year)	
Tax Code†	200H
Amended code†	300H
Week/Month no. in which applied	S
Year to 5 April 19......	

National Insurance Contributions *

MONTH number	WEEK number	Total of Employer's and Employee's Contributions payable 1a	Employee's contributions payable 1b	Employee's contributions at Contracted-out rate included in Col. 1b 1c	Statutory sick pay in the week or month included in col. 2 1d	Pay in the week or month including statutory sick pay 2	Total pay to date 3	Total free pay to date as shown by Table A 4	Total taxable pay to date 5	Total tax due to date as shown by Taxable Pay Tables 6	Tax deducted or refunded in the week or month Mark refunds "R" 7	For employer's use
6 April to 5 May	1	16 94	7 22			80 00	80 00	38 64	41 36	12 30	12 30	
	2	16 94	7 22			80 00	160 00	77 28	82 72	24 60	12 30	
	3	16 94	7 22			80 00	240 00	115 92	124 08	37 20	12 60	
1	4	16 94	7 22			80 00	320 00	154 56	165 44	49 50	12 30	
6 May to 5 June	5	16 94	7 22			80 00	400 00	289 35	110 65	33 00	16 50	R
	6					80 00						
2	7											
6 June to 5 July	8											
	9											
	10											
3	11											
6 July to 5 Aug	12											
	13											
	14											
4	15											
6 Aug to 5 Sept	16											
	17											
	18											
5	19											
6 Sept to 5 Oct	20											
	21											
	22											
6	23											
6 Oct to 5 Nov	24											
	25											
	26											
7	27											
	28											
	29											
	30											

Total carried forward | Total carried forward | Total carried forward | Total carried forward | Total carried forward

PAYE Income Tax

*N.I. Contribution Table letter must be entered overleaf beside the N.I. totals boxes – see the note shown there.

This box may be used if the employer wishes to record the N.I. letter while this side of the sheet is in use

† If amended cross out previous code

ø If in any week/month the amount in column 4 is more than the amount in column 3, make no entry in column 5.

P11
(New)

SPECIMEN

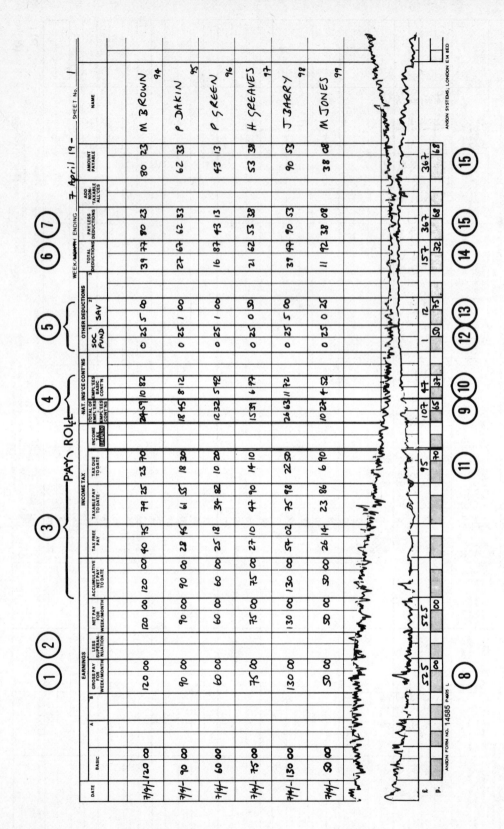

Fig 48 Payroll

At this stage the employee's pay record sheet (Fig 49, p 130) and pay slip (Fig 50, p 131) are completed; examples shown are for Mr M Brown.

When the information relating to the pay of all employees has been entered the payroll is totalled as follows:

Payroll Ref No

Earnings Providing the total gross pay for all employees. — 8

Combined National Insurance contributions The employee's and employer's contributions are calculated. Each week the Inland Revenue account is credited with these amounts and the wages account debited. The contributions are paid once a month to the Board of Inland Revenue. — 9

Employee's National Insurance contributions The total of the employee's national insurance is a deduction from gross pay (8) and together with the total of the employer's national insurance provides the figure arrived at in (9). — 10

Income tax Each week the Inland Revenue account is credited with the amount deducted for income tax (less any amounts refunded). The employer holds this total until the end of the month when he pays it to the Board of Inland Revenue. — 11

Social fund The total deducted is paid to the Treasurer of the Social Fund and credited to the bank account. — 12

Savings The total is paid to a savings account and credited to the bank account. — 13

Records of the individual employees' savings are kept by trustees of the savings fund.

Total deductions The total of this column must equal the totals of columns 10, 11, 12 and 13 for the employees' deductions. This work, referred to as cross-casting, is an essential check on the accuracy of the work of the wages clerks. — 14

Net payment This is the total sum which must be drawn from the bank for payment of wages and it must equal the gross pay (8) less total deductions (14) – another check on the accuracy of the calculations. — 15

The number of coins and notes required for each employee is calculated and totalled, an exercise known as 'coining'. The total pay for the six employees listed on the payroll on p 128 is £367.68 which is calculated in the coining summary (Fig 51, p 131) and withdrawn from the bank in the appropriate notes and coins, as in the cash summary on p 131.

After collection from the bank the cash is sorted into the required amounts in accordance with the pay slips. The money is not inserted into the packets until the total has been sorted correctly and the amounts re-checked by a second member of staff. The employees call at the wages office to collect and sign for their pay packets.

The procedure outlined above is suitable for the payment of wages in cash when the entries are made manually. For the payment by cheque, credit transfer or National Giro and when computers are employed there will be variations in the procedure used. See Unit 14.3 relating to the use of computers.

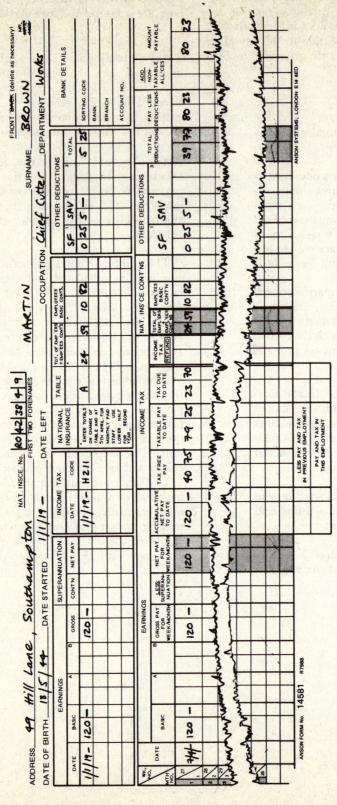

Fig 49 Pay record sheet

DATE	BASIC	A	B	GROSS PAY FOR WEEK/MONTH	LESS. SUPERAN- NUATION	NET PAY FOR WEEK/MONTH	ACCUMULATIVE NET PAY TO DATE	TAX FREE PAY	TAXABLE PAY TO DATE	TAX DUE TO DATE	INCOME TAX REFUND
7/4/-	120 -			120 -		120 -	120 -	40 75	79 25	23 70	

EMPL'EES BASIC CONT'N	SF [1]	SAV [2]	[3]	TOTAL DEDUCTIONS	PAY LESS DEDUCTIONS	ADD: NON- TAXABLE ALL'CES	AMOUNT PAYABLE	NAME
10.82	0 25	5 -		39 77	80 23		80 23	M BROWN 94

Fig 50   Pay slip

Net payments £	£10	£5	£1	50p	20p	10p	5p	2p	1p
80.23	8				1			1	1
62.33	6		2		1	1		1	1
43.13	4		3			1		1	1
53.38	5		3		1	1	1	1	1
90.53	9			1				1	1
38.08	3	1	3				1	1	1
367.68	35	1	11	1	3	3	2	6	6

Fig 51   Coining summary

Cash summary:

```
          £
 35 @ £10 = 350.00
  1 @ £5  =   5.00
 11 @ £1  =  11.00
  1 @ 50p =   0.50
  3 @ 20p =   0.60
  3 @ 10p =   0.30
  2 @  5p =   0.10
  6 @  2p =   0.12
  6 @  1p =   0.06
              ──────
              367.68
              ══════
```

Payroll totals as given in the payroll on page 128

Gross pay £	Employer's National Insurance £	Total National Insurance £	Income Tax £	Social Fund £	Savings £	Net pay £
525.00	60.28	107.65	95.70	1.50	12.75	367.68

Wages Account

Details	Ref	Dr £	Cr £	Bal £
Employer's NI	11	60.28		60.28
Gross pay	8	525.00		585.28

Inland Revenue Account

Details	Ref	Dr £	Cr £	Bal £
Income tax	11		95.70	95.70
National Insurance	9		*107.65	203.35 Cr

Bank Account

Details	Ref	Dr £	Cr £	Bal £
Net pay	15		367.68	367.68
Savings	13		12.75	380.43
Social fund			1.50	381.93 Cr

Debits: Wages Account = £585.28

£585.28

Credits: Bank Account = £381.93

Inland Revenue Account = £203.35

£585.28

* Any statutory sick pay paid out is deducted from National Insurance before this is paid to Inland Revenue.

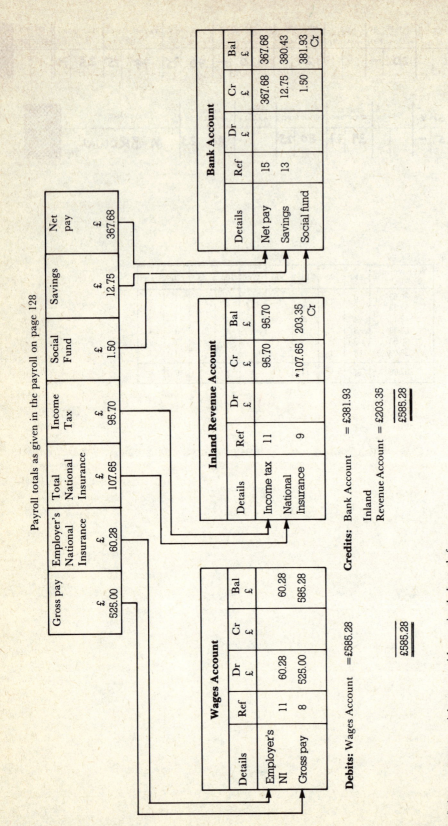

Fig 52 Procedure for posting wages

Exercises

1 Prepare the employees' individual pay records, payroll and pay slips for weeks 2, 3 and 4 for the following employees whose week 1 pay details were given on p 128.

Employee	Code No	Gross pay Week 2	Week 3	Week 4
		£	£	£
M Brown	211H	120.00	125.00	125.00
P Dakin	147L	90.00	65.00	90.00
P Green	130L	60.00	62.00	62.00
H Greaves	140L	80.00	80.00	80.00
J Barry	280H	130.00	130.00	134.00
M Jones	135L	60.00	60.00	60.00

Social fund and savings contributions remain the same as for week 1.

2 *a* Make out a cash analysis showing what you will collect from the bank to pay the following wages:

£	£	£
62.25	75.16	120.45
105.14	110.23	60.84
48.99	78.11	105.26

  b What statutory deductions must be made from wages?

  c How are national insurance contributions calculated and entered?

3 You are the general clerk of a retail store employing four shop assistants who are paid in cash weekly, one week in arrears. The net wages for the week ending Saturday 20 June 19— which will be paid on Friday 26 June 19— are as follows:

	£
T Bell	52.79
R Carter	63.14
T King	55.18
R Telman	68.10

You are required to calculate the number and denominations of coins and notes required to pay the wages of the four men. The owner of the business will not pay with notes greater than £5 and insists that at least one £1 note should be present in every pay packet. *(RSA BKI)*

4 The following table refers to two employees:

Name	Hours worked w/e 18 June	Rate £
John Brown	42	2.00
Wilson Cap	46	1.50

Their employment has a basic working week of 40 hours, and all overtime is paid at time and a half. Income tax is paid as follows: Brown £5, Cap £3; 5% of gross earnings is to be deducted for social security contributions. All employees make a voluntary contribution towards the social and athletic club of £1.00 per week.

You are required to calculate the net pay of each employee and set out pay slips for the week ending 18 June 19—. *(RSA BKI)*

14 Computerised accounts

The manual procedures for recording ledger accounts can be speeded up and more information supplied if a computer is used. A wide variety of computers are available, ranging from the small 'personal' computers with limited memory capacities to the mainframe computers used by large business concerns. For the purposes of this book we shall consider the operation of a typical microcomputer which is likely to be in use in a small business such as Faulkners. Whatever their size computers have certain common features, such as:

VDU – a visual display unit. This is the screen which displays information to the operator and provides instructions to lead him through the process of computing.

Keyboard – similar to a typewriter keyboard (the input) used to enter data into the computer and through which the operator gives instructions to the computer.

CPU – a central processing unit – containing the control unit, the main store and the arithmetic/logic unit. This is the electronic 'brain' which manipulates data.

Printer – for printing information (the output).
Backing storage – magnetic floppy discs (approximately 120 A4 pages on an 8″ or 5¼″ disc) or hard discs (approximately 40 times the amount stored on a floppy disc).

The physical parts of a computer, ie the CPU and the printer are known as **hardware** whereas the programs and data are the **software**. The program is an essential ingredient in computing as it provides a list of instructions without which the computer cannot perform any operations.

Once the program is switched on it is necessary to key in the date, after which a menu appears on the screen. **Menu** is the name given to the list of operations which may be selected. The main menus contain the various options or functions which can be performed, and these are further subdivided into the specific tasks, eg if a credit note has to be entered in a supplier's account the main menu **1** (enter transaction) is selected followed by the sub-menu **3** (credit notes).

14.1 Purchases

Typical menus and sub-menus for transactions involving purchases might include:

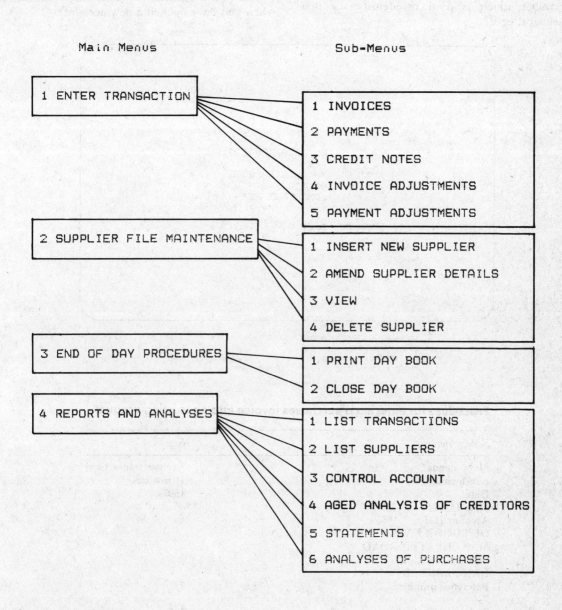

Main Menus

Sub-Menus

1 ENTER TRANSACTION

1 INVOICES

2 PAYMENTS

3 CREDIT NOTES

4 INVOICE ADJUSTMENTS

5 PAYMENT ADJUSTMENTS

2 SUPPLIER FILE MAINTENANCE

1 INSERT NEW SUPPLIER

2 AMEND SUPPLIER DETAILS

3 VIEW

4 DELETE SUPPLIER

3 END OF DAY PROCEDURES

1 PRINT DAY BOOK

2 CLOSE DAY BOOK

4 REPORTS AND ANALYSES

1 LIST TRANSACTIONS

2 LIST SUPPLIERS

3 CONTROL ACCOUNT

4 AGED ANALYSIS OF CREDITORS

5 STATEMENTS

6 ANALYSES OF PURCHASES

Procedure for opening a new account

When a new account has to be opened the operator keys in **2** (Supplier file maintenance) followed by **1** for the sub-menu (Insert new supplier) and is then instructed to key in further items of information:

a the account ID – this is the account reference number which is used to identify the new account, eg P1

b the supplier's name and address

c opening balance – if one is being transferred from a manual system

The operator has to check the entries on the screen before operating the 'return' key to store them on the disc.

The VDU shows the following information when you have opened a new account:

```
ID       P1

NAME     OUTDOOR FABRICS PLC

ADDRESS  MANCHESTER ROAD
         BOLTON
         LANCS BN3 2BT


BALANCE  0.00
```

Procedure for entering a purchases invoice into an existing account

Screen shows	Key in
Main menus	1 (enter transaction)
Sub-menus	1 (invoices)
Date?	1507–
Date 15/07/–	
Account ID?	P1
OUTDOOR FABRICS PLC	
MANCHESTER ROAD	
BOLTON	
LANCS BN3 2BT	
Reference number?	73
73	
Their invoice number?	437
437	
Description	Invoice
INVOICE	
Total price?	260.47
260.47	

The VDU and print-out if required, shows the following information

```
                    PURCHASES LEDGER

   DATE  15/07/--

   ACCOUNT ID  P1

   NAME        OUTDOOR FABRICS PLC

   ADDRESS     MANCHESTER ROAD.
               BOLTON
               LANCS BN3 2BT

   DATE       REF  INV NO   DESCRIPTION      DEBIT    CREDIT

   01/07/--                 BALANCE AT START          00.00

   15/07/--   437   73      INVOICE                   260.47

                            BALANCE AT END            260.47

              CURRENT    30 DAYS      60 DAYS      90 DAYS

              260.47
```

Procedure for entering payment into an existing account

Screen shows	Key in
Main menus	1 (enter transactions)
Sub-menus	2 (payments)
Date?	15088–
Date 15/08/8–	
Print advice notes?	Y (for yes)
Account ID?	P1
OUTDOOR FABRICS PLC	
MANCHESTER ROAD	
BOLTON	
LANCS BN3 2BT	
Cheque no?	729
729	
Invoice no?	73
73	
Date 15/07/–	
Outstanding 260.47	
Pay?	Y
260.47 OK?	Y
FULL SETTLEMENT	

The VDU and print-out if required, shows the
following information:

```
                           PURCHASES LEDGER
  DATE 15/08/--

  ACCOUNT ID  P1

  NAME  OUTDOOR FABRICS PLC

  ADDRESS  MANCHESTER ROAD, BOLTON, LANCS. BN3 2BT

  YEAR TO DATE    260.47

  REF     DATE    INV NO     DESCRIPTION      DEBIT      CREDIT

                           BALANCE AT START              00.00

  437   15/07/--    73      INVOICE                      260.47

  437   15/08/--   729      PAYMENT          260.47

                           BALANCE AT END                00.00

  CURRENT            30 DAYS          60 DAYS          90 DAYS

  ASSIGNED    00.00
```

Purchases ledger reports

One of the advantages of a computer is its ability to
provide reports with useful information for the
accounts department. The following are examples
of the reports which can be extracted from the
computer memory:

1 Purchases Ledger Account listing

This provides details of the suppliers' accounts
with the totals of the amounts owing by the firm, as
well as the total of all purchases made during the
year (to date).

The example for P Faulkner & Sons is shown
opposite.

```
   PURCHASE LEDGER ACCOUNT LISTING ON 15/07/-
ACC. ID      NAME          BALANCE YEAR TOT. CURRENT OVER 30 OVER 60 OVER 90
   P1 OUTDOOR FABRICS PLC    260.47   260.47  260.47    0.00    0.00    0.00
   P2 FETTLENOLD & SONS      550.00  2550.00  550.00    0.00    0.00    0.00
   P3 DARLING & SONS           8.36   110.00    8.36    0.00    0.00    0.00
   P4 NKG PLC                 0.00    500.00    0.00    0.00    0.00    0.00
   P5 INSULATION SUPPLY CO. LTD 120.00 200.00   0.00  120.00    0.00    0.00
      TOTALS                938.83  3620.47  818.83  120.00    0.00    0.00
```

2 Purchase Ledger analysis on 15/07/—

```
   NO   DESCRIPTION        DEBIT        CREDIT
   10   ALUMINIUM TUBING   1207.00
   11   FOAM                620.00
   12   NYLON (PROOFED)     325.00
   13   PVC                1014.00
   14   SPRINGS             807.50
   15   TENT CLOTHS        3200.00
   16   ZIPS                300.00
  101   BANK ACCOUNT                   7655.67
  103   VAT CONTROL        1121.00
  106   CREDITORS CONTROL               938.83
        TOTALS            8594.50      8594.50
```

14.2 Sales

The menus for the Sales Ledger are similar to those used for the Purchases Ledger, but with the addition of invoice, credit note and statement preparation. The Sales Ledger Accounts are updated simultaneously with the preparation of the invoices and credit notes. Up-to-date statements can be printed at any time during the financial period.

Other Sales Ledger sub-menus are used for:

a preparing credit notes and entering them into customers' accounts
b entering receipts in customers' accounts
c printing statements
d printing Sales Day Books and Sales Returns Day Books
e printing cash and VAT accounts and analysis
f sales analyses

Procedure for preparing an invoice and entering it into an existing account

Screen shows	Key in
Main menus	1 (enter transaction)
Sub-menus	1 (invoices)
1624 (the next number)	
Account ID?	14
BRENTFORDS PLC	
WESTON HOUSE	
PICCADILLY	
LONDON W1V 9PA	
Date of invoice?	08078–
8/07/8—	
Order no?	S63729
FAULKNER MAJOR FRAME TENTS	
QUANTITY 60	
CAT NO 734T	
PRICE EACH 260.00	
TOTAL PRICE 15600.00	
Trade discount?	15
2340.00	
VAT standard rate? Y or N	Y
1989.00	
Total? Y or N	Y
15 249.00	

This is the amount debited to the customer's account. If the credit limit has been exceeded this will be shown automatically.

Print invoice? Y or N   Y

The customer's account is debited with the amount of the invoice.

14.3 Wages

Typical menus and sub-menus for wages applications include the following:

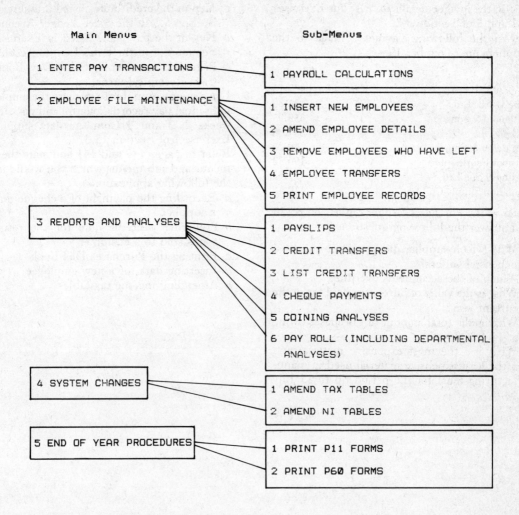

Main Menus	Sub-Menus
1 ENTER PAY TRANSACTIONS	1 PAYROLL CALCULATIONS
2 EMPLOYEE FILE MAINTENANCE	1 INSERT NEW EMPLOYEES 2 AMEND EMPLOYEE DETAILS 3 REMOVE EMPLOYEES WHO HAVE LEFT 4 EMPLOYEE TRANSFERS 5 PRINT EMPLOYEE RECORDS
3 REPORTS AND ANALYSES	1 PAYSLIPS 2 CREDIT TRANSFERS 3 LIST CREDIT TRANSFERS 4 CHEQUE PAYMENTS 5 COINING ANALYSES 6 PAY ROLL (INCLUDING DEPARTMENTAL ANALYSES)
4 SYSTEM CHANGES	1 AMEND TAX TABLES 2 AMEND NI TABLES
5 END OF YEAR PROCEDURES	1 PRINT P11 FORMS 2 PRINT P60 FORMS

When an 'exception' payroll is used only non-standard payments and deductions need to be input into the system; the employees automatically receive their basic pay and their normal standard deductions such as union subscriptions, savings etc.

Weekly or monthly payroll calculations are performed on Menu 1 (Enter pay transactions) as follows:

1 Previous pay, tax details, etc, held on the employee master file, are brought forward.
2 Gross pay is calculated and entered.
3 Income tax is calculated and entered.
4 National Insurance contributions for employer and employee are calculated and entered.
5 Deductions in 2 and 3 and any other deductions are totalled and deducted from gross pay to arrive at net pay.
6 The employee master file is updated with the entries made in 2, 3, 4 and 5.

These calculations can then be printed on the appropriate forms by switching over to the following sub-menus:

3.1 pay slips
3.5 coining analyses
3.6 payroll

Exercises

1 Using a microcomputer open accounts for the eight suppliers given in the material/suppliers index on p 5 on 19 September 19—.

2 Key-in the invoice details on p 18 for Exercises 1, 2 and 3 of Section 3.2.

3 Key-in the following payments made to the suppliers on 7 October 19—:

	£
NKG plc	1 427.15
Tape Works Ltd	36.80
Fettlenold & Sons	359.95
CIC plc	851.80
Sam Beller & Sons	40.25
Outdoor Fabrics plc	190.32
Darling & Son Ltd	171.92
Insulation Supply Co Ltd	110.40

4 Refer to the Purchases Ledger reports on p 139 and answer the following questions:

a With which supplier did you place the most expensive orders?

b Which of the accounts is overdue?

c What is the value of purchases paid for in the current year?

d What is the total amount of purchases owing at 15 July 19—?

e What is i the most expensive material and ii the least expensive material used in manufacturing tents for the period up to 15 July 19—?

5 a Using a microcomputer open accounts for the ten customers contained in Exercise 1a of Section 5.5.

b Key-in the invoices listed in Exercises 2–5 of Section 5.2 in the Sales Ledger Accounts.

c Key-in the credit notes listed in Exercise 1 of Section 5.3 in the Sales Ledger Accounts.

d Key-in the payments listed in Exercise 5 of Section 5.4 in the Sales Ledger Accounts.

e Print the statements, Sales Day Book and Cash Receipts Journal.

6 Use a microcomputer to prepare the employees' individual pay records, payroll and pay slips for weeks 2, 3 and 4 from the data supplied in Exercise 1 of Section 13.3.

7 Refer to pages 135 and 141 and state the main menus and sub-menus which you would use for the following applications:

a Recording the payment of a cheque made to a supplier

b Preparing a credit note for the return of goods sold to a customer

c Printing the Purchases Day Book

d Inserting data for a new employee

e Amending income tax tables

15 Accounts for non-trading concerns

There are many organisations which do not trade for profit and exist in order to provide activities for those who choose to belong to them such as cricket clubs, professional societies, churches, youth clubs and social clubs. Nevertheless they are involved in receiving income (very often in the form of membership subscriptions and donations) and paying expenses and must, therefore, keep some form of financial records. The records may be no more than a summary of the Cash Book called a Receipts and Payments Account and/or, if a more formal record is required by the rules or the members, an Income and Expenditure Account (with or without a Balance Sheet).

Receipts and Payments Account

This account, illustrated on p 144, is a summary of cash received and paid during a given period and it shows the amount of cash in hand at the end of the period.

Procedure:
1 The account should begin with the balance of cash held at the beginning of the period which will be the same as the closing balance of cash for the previous period.
2 The receipts are listed under appropriate headings, summarised, totalled and *added* to the opening balance of cash in **1**.
3 The payments are listed under appropriate headings, summarised, totalled and *deducted* from the total receipts calculated in **2**.
4 The final total in **3** provides the balance of cash at the end of the period which should agree with the amount of cash in hand.

Income and Expenditure Account

This account, illustrated on p 145, is similar to a Trading/Profit and Loss Account, but instead of calculating net profit and adding it to the capital account balance in a Balance Sheet, the excess of

income over expenditure is called a surplus and this is added to an accumulated fund in the Balance Sheet. If the expenditure exceeds the income the resulting 'loss' is called a deficit and this is deducted from an accumulated fund in the Balance Sheet. The income includes all that is due (whether it is paid or not) for the period covered by the account and likewise the expenditure allows for accruals and prepayments.

Procedure:
1 If a closing cash figure is not given prepare a receipts and payments account containing only actual *cash* receipts and payments.
2 Convert the Receipts and Payments Account into an Income and Expenditure Account by:
   a allowing for prepayments and accruals (especially subscriptions owing)
   b including only *revenue* expenditure and income: any capital expenditure (eg the purchase of a typewriter) or capital income (loans to the organisation) should not be included and should be placed in the Balance Sheet.
3 Calculate a net total for each item of income and expenditure; this may entail the compilation of a small Receipts and Payments Account or it may even require a Trading Account, as in the case of refreshments on p 145.
4 List all items of income and total them.
5 List all items of expenditure, deducting prepayments and adding accruals, and total them.
6 Deduct the total expenditure from the total income to arrive at a surplus or a deficit.
7 If a Balance Sheet is required:
   a list and total the assets
   b list and total the liabilities and subtract them from the assets
   c calculate the opening accumulated fund balance by deducting the liabilities from the assets at the commencement of the period
   d add the surplus or deduct the deficit from the opening accumulated fund balance to arrive at the closing accumulated fund balance. This should be the same as the answer in *b*, ie assets minus liabilities

Mr P Faulkner encouraged his staff to meet together socially in the firm's Staff Association to promote good relationships between staff and maintain a high standard of morale. To this end he gave a grant of £200 each year. On 1 April 19— the Staff Association's records contained the following entries:

	£
Cash in hand	210.00
Stock of refreshments	75.00
A creditor (Catering Supplies Ltd) for refreshments supplied	26.00

During the following year to 31 March 19— the Honorary Secretary and Treasurer received and paid the following amounts:

Receipts	£	Payments	£
Grant from Mr Faulkner	200.00	Part-time cleaner's wages	300.00
Subscriptions	50.00	Cleaning materials	36.00
Whist drive proceeds	271.00	Suppliers of refreshments	250.00
Sale of refreshments	440.00	Rent of rooms	312.00
Disco proceeds	175.00	New typewriter	120.00
		Telephone, stationery, etc	74.00

At the end of the financial year the club owed £46 to Catering Supplies Ltd for refreshments supplied and had £20 of refreshments in stock.

The Income and Expenditure Account and Balance Sheet were prepared to present to the members at the annual general meeting to be held on 10 April 19—. However, the following workings **1**, **2** and **3** are necessary in order to prepare the Income and Expenditure Account and a Balance Sheet:

**1   Faulkner's Staff Association
Receipts and Payments Account
for the year ended 31 March 19—**

	£	£
Balance of cash in hand (1 April 19—)		210.00
Add Receipts:		
Grant	200.00	
Subscriptions	50.00	
Whist drive proceeds	271.00	
Sale of refreshments	440.00	
Disco proceeds	175.00	
		1 136.00
		1 346.00
Less Payments:		
Part-time cleaner's wages	300.00	
Cleaning materials	36.00	
Refreshment supplies	250.00	
Rent of rooms	312.00	
New typewriter	120.00	
Telephone, stationery etc	74.00	
		1 092.00
Balance of cash in hand (31 March 19—)		254.00

2 **Accumulated fund at 1 April 19—**

(Assets – Liabilities)

Cash in hand	210.00
Stock	75.00
	285.00
Less Creditor	26.00
	259.00

---

3 **Calculation of profit or loss on sale of refreshments**

	£	£	£
Sale of refreshments			440.00
Less Cost of refreshments:			
Opening stock		75.00	
Add Purchases paid	250.00		
Purchases owing (31/3/19—)	46.00		
	296.00		
Less Amount owing for purchases at beginning of year	26.00		
		270.00	
		345.00	
Less Closing stock		20.00	
			325.00
Net proceeds from sale of refreshments			115.00

Faulkner's Staff Association
Income and Expenditure Account
for the year ended 31 March 19—

Income	£	£
Grant from P Faulkner & Sons	200.00	
Subscriptions	50.00	
Whist drive proceeds	271.00	
Refreshments sale proceeds	115.00	
Disco proceeds	175.00	
		811.00
Less **Expenditure**		
Part-time cleaner's wages	300.00	
Cleaning materials	36.00	
Rent of rooms	312.00	
Telephone, stationery etc	74.00	
		722.00
Surplus for the year		89.00

Balance Sheet as at 31 March 19—

	£	£
Assets		
New typewriter	120.00	
Stock of refreshments	20.00	
Cash in hand	254.00	
		394.00
Less **Liabilities**		
Creditor: Catering Supplies Ltd		46.00
		348.00
Accumulated fund (1 April 19—)	259.00	
Add Surplus for the year	89.00	
		348.00

Exercises

1 The Shockers Cricket Club was formed on 1 April 19—. From their Receipts and Payments Account shown below, you are required to prepare:

    a an Income and Expenditure Account for the year ended 31 March 19—

    b a Balance Sheet as at that date

Receipts and Payments Account (year ended 31 March 19—)

	£		£
Loans from members @ 8% per annum	450	Bar refreshments purchased	203
Bar takings	246	Purchase of lockers for players	180
Subscriptions from members	540	Travelling expenses	96
Match receipts	114	Printing	48
		Stationery and postage	28
		Rent	225
		Cricket League fees	69
		Rates and insurance	150
		Purchase of sporting equipment	152
		Balance c/d	199
	1 350		1 350

Notes at 31 March 19—:

a A stationery bill of £6 is outstanding

b There were bar stocks valued at £48

c The interest on loans from members was due for the full year ended 31 March 19—

d Rent was prepaid into the forthcoming year £25

e £80 is to be paid to the Club Treasurer for his services   (RSA BKI)

2 The Parkington Social Club meets during the evenings in rented accommodation. On 1 June 19— its assets and liabilities were:

	£
Cash in hand	410
Stocks of food etc	75
Creditor for food supplied	36

During the year to 31 May— the club received and paid the amounts shown below. On 31 May 19— the club owed £40 for food supplied, but all stocks had been sold.

You are required to:

a Calculate the accumulated fund on 1 June 19—

b Calculate the amount of cash which should be in hand on 31 May 19—

c Prepare an Income and Expenditure Account for the year ended 31 May 19—

d Set out a Balance Sheet as at 31 May 19—   (RSA BKI)

Receipts		*Payments*	
	£		£
Subscriptions	1 740	Cleaners' wages	950
Jumble sales	871	Cleaning materials	76
Sales of food etc	440	Payments to suppliers of food etc	350
		Rent and rates	750
		Typewriter for secretary's use	610
		Secretarial expenses	310

3 The following is a list of the receipts and payments made by the treasurer of the Mayfield Social Club during the year ended 31 May 19—:

	£
Balance at bank 1 June 198—	850
Subscriptions received during year	1 200
Profit on sale of refreshments	410
Proceeds of whist drives and dances	175
Rent of hall paid during year	220
Purchase of new games equipment (regarded as revenue expenditure)	210
Cleaners' wages	520
Heating and lighting payments	175
Secretarial expenses	500
Purchase of new furniture	400

The following items are due for the year ended 31 May 19— but have not yet been paid:

	£
Rent of hall for one month	20
An electricity account for lighting	25

You are to prepare:
a The Mayfield Social Club's Receipts and Payments Account for the year ended 31 May 19—
b The Mayfield Social Club's Income and Expenditure Account for the year ended 31 May 19— (*RSA BKI*)

4 The assets and liabilities of the Greenlands Dancing Club as at 1 January 19— were:

	£
Balance at bank	460
Equipment	380
Rent of hall owing	50
Stock of stationery	15

Below is a summary of the receipts and payments of the club for the year ended 31 December 19—. The following additional information is provided:

a Stock of stationery at 31 December 19— was £20
b Rent of hall owing at 31 December 19— £60
Required:

i A calculation of the accumulated fund as at 1 January 19—
ii An Income and Expenditure Account for the year ended 31 December 19— showing clearly the profit/loss on the raffles and on the annual dinner dance
iii A Balance Sheet as at 31 December 19— (*RSA BKI*)

Receipts	£	Payments	£
Balance 1/1/19—	460	Purchase of new equipment	250
Annual dinner dance	500	Rent of hall	550
Sale of raffle tickets	435	Expenses of annual dinner dance	560
Subscriptions	80	Stationery	40
Takings at the door	1 030	Raffle prizes	215
		Balance	890
	2 505		2 505

Abbreviated answers

Unit	Exercise 1		Exercise 2

Unit

1   *a* £50 000

     b 20p profit, 26p materials, 26p wages, 20p admin, 8p distrbn

2.1

3.1   *a* £229.77, *b* £1 932.00, *c* £196.96

3.3   Total £1 729.02, Goods £1 447.00, Carr £56.50, VAT £225.52

3.4   Total £223.21, Goods £194.10, VAT £29.11

3.5   *a* reverse Dr and Cr entries; all Cr balances
     b CPJ £682.39

3.6   VAT £587.32, Goods £3 915.50, Cash —, Bal £5 092.82, Old Bal £590.00

3.7   £12 421.29

5.1   Aldous £894.07, Baldwin £4 034.80, Coleman £20 882.44

5.2   Total £20 067.37, Goods £17 507.00, VAT £2 560.37

5.3   *b* Total £66.70, Goods £58.00, VAT £8.70

5.4   Chudleigh £924.00, Dreamland £225.50

5.5   *b*

VAT (£)	Goods (£)	Cash (£)	Bal (£)	Old Bal (£)
207.67	1 420.33	—	1 628.00	—
212.72	1 454.88	—	2 484.90	817.30
352.20	2 408.80	—	4 983.00	2 222.00
1 174.16	8 029.54	—	14 194.40	4 990.70

c

(8.70)	(58.00)	—	4 298.10	4 364.80

d

		1 192.40	9 026.25	10 218.65
		990.00	1 013.10	2 003.10
		2 743.18	8 307.85	11 051.03
		6 978.72	99.95	7 078.67

5.6   £6 784.41

5.7   Total £1 667.60, Tents £277.35, S'bags £422.08, R'sacks £461.61, C'beds £293.84, VAT £212.72

6.1   CRJ £1 153.15, CPJ £705.65, CPJ (Ex) £247.40, Bal £2 938.40

6.2   Total £1 192.40

6.3   Cash Book bal (with amendments) £767.40

6.4   Total expenditure £33.46, Bal £16.54

Exercise 2

£4 per student

300

£346.23

Total £1 459.57, Goods £1 228.30, Carr £40.90, VAT £190.37

a Details of goods sold to M Menton and returned by M Menton

b Balance £72.00 Cr

a Wilkinson

b **1** is Dr invoices, **2** is Cr payments/discounts/allowances, **3** is balance owing by Joyce

c Debtor Joyce, creditor Wilkinson, £327.50

VAT (£)	Goods (£)	Cash (£)	Bal (£)	Old Bal (£)
437.69	2 918.03	—	7 947.94	4 592.22
365.87	2 439.32	—	9 580.69	6 775.50
437.25	2 915.00	—	17 603.04	14 250.79
(5.25)	(35.00)	—	6 432.55	6 472.80
—	—	390.00	6 670.14	7 060.14

£6 843.00

Arnold £180.53, Attwood £3 480.01, Bell £12 714.78, Brown £257.90, Charles £144.42, Coleman £3 289.73

Total £1 628.00, Goods £1 420.33, VAT £207.67

SDB: Total £229.19, Goods £199.30, VAT £29.89

SRB: Total £43.70, Goods £38.00, VAT £5.70

£737.80

VAT (£)	Goods (£)	Cash (£)	Bal (£)	Old Bal (£)
197.98	1 320.02	—	2 599.00	1 081.00
—	—	557.00	648.00	1 205.00
(4.30)	(28.70)	—	986.00	1 019.00
111.76	745.14	—	1 751.90	895.00
—	—	820.00	1 111.00	1 931.00
81.06	540.44	—	1 626.40	1 004.90

£2 737.40

Total £20 067.37, Tents £16 998.50, R'sacks £225.00, C'beds £283.50, VAT £2 560.37

Bank A/c bal £1 860.91

Total £100.35

£213.00

Total expenditure £38.25, Bal £11.75

Exercise 1

7 *a* Bad debt Dr, T Warren Cr
  b Machinery/plant Dr, Steel Makers Cr
  c Drawings Dr, R Browning Cr
  d Disc rec'd Dr, P Shelley Cr
8 £9 470.00
9 £11 550.00
10 *a* 900 units
  b Cost of sales £5 200, Gr prof £2 550
11 Gr prof £7 047, N prof £2 607
12 Capital A/c bal £26 000, B/S total £32 000
13.1 Adams £92.40, Smith £111.60, Spinks £81.60, Williams
  £98.40

13.2*

Week	1	2	3	4
I tax (£)	13.20	13.50	13.50	13.50
N I (£)	6.32	6.32	6.32	6.32

Week	5	6	7	8
I tax (£)	15.00	14.70	—	—
N I (£)	6.77	6.77	—	—

Week	9	10	11	12
I tax (£)	16.50	4.80	15.30	14.70
N I (£)	7.22	7.22	7.22	7.04

13.3*

	Wk 2 (£)	Wk 3 (£)	Wk 4 (£)
Brown	80.23	83.28	82.98
Dakin	62.03	47.08	62.03
Green	42.83	44.05	44.05
Greaves	56.13	56.13	56.13
Barry	90.23	90.23	92.67
Jones	43.88	43.88	43.88

14
15 Surplus £32.00, B/S £32.00

* Using 1982/83 tax tables and 1983 NI tables

Exercise 2

Office Furniture Dr, Crescent Furniture Cr
Bad debts Dr, P Richards Cr
J Belling Dr, J Bell Cr
Car Traders Dr, Motor vehicles Cr
£5 610.00
£3 570.00
Net purchases £18 040, Cost of goods offered for sale £19 500,
Cost of sales £22 000, Net sales £30 000, Gr prof £8 000
Gr prof £19 650, N prof £6 400
N prof £5 000, B/S total £44 300
£165.90

Week	24	25	26	27
I tax (£)	15.30	13.50	15.00	14.70
N I (£)	8.12	8.12	8.48	8.48

Week	28	29	30
I tax (£)	33.60R	13.20	1.20R
N I (£)	8.48	8.48	4.16

a		
£10	730
£5	25
£1	8
50p	1
20p	1.60
10p	0.40
5p	0.25
2p	0.14
1p	0.04
	£766.43

b N I & I tax

c DHSS tables or % entered on tax
  deduction card

See **3.2**
a £449.00, *b* £415.00, *c* £536.00 surplus *d* £985.00

Index